You Invited Me In…

Other Works by Dr. John Wagner

How to Be a More Effective Personal Witness

You Invited Me In...

The Story of a Pentecostal Hospitality House Military Ministry

Dr. John and Yvonne Wagner

LIGHTHOUSE MILITARY MINISTRY

Copyright (c) 2018   Dr. John and Yvonne Wagner

All rights reserved. No part of this book may be used or reproduced by any means, graphic, electronic, or mechanical, including photocopying, recording, taping or by any information storage retrieval system without the written permission of the author except in the use of brief quotations embodied in critical articles and reviews.

Unless otherwise indicated, all scripture quotations are from The Holy Bible, New International Version®, NIV® Copyright ©1973, 1978, 1984, 2011 by Biblica, Inc.® Used by permission. All rights reserved worldwide.

Scripture quotations marked NIRV are from the New International Reader's Version (NIRV), Copyright © 1995, 1996, 1998, 2014 by Biblica, Inc.®. Used by permission. All rights reserved worldwide.

Scripture quotations marked ESV are from the ESV® Bible (The Holy Bible, English Standard Version®), copyright © 2001 by Crossway, a publishing ministry of Good News Publishers. Used by permission. All rights reserved.

Scripture quotations marked KJV are from the Holy Bible, King James Version.

Cover design by author.

To learn more about or to purchase, this or other works by
Dr. John Wagner, go to:
http://lighthousemilitaryministry.org
or
http://amazon.com/author/john-wagner

ISBN: 978-1-948773-22-5
Library of Congress Control Number: 2018909293

Dedication

Forty-seven years ago, as a 19 year old seaman in the United States Navy, I was invited to a "party" at a Christian servicemen's center where I met a young woman who had the conviction that she would not date a non-Christian. It was through her witness and the ministry of the *Port O' Call* that I found Jesus Christ as my Savior. Two years later that young woman and I were married and for 45 years have been partners in ministry.

In 1999 we began praying about the possibility of moving to Virginia Beach to minister to young military men and women. Then in March of 2000 Yvonne's mother went to be with the Lord. It was through the inheritance she left Yvonne that we were financially able to make the transition from Grand Junction, Colorado to Virginia Beach, Virginia. I will always consider Trude Silver the benefactress who the Lord used to make this ministry possible. Her frugality and savings are now being invested in the lives of young military men and women.

When I considered pursuing the Doctor of Ministry degree at Regent University to gain the knowledge and skills for the benefit of our ministry, the financial aspect was again a significant part of the decision. Yvonne volunteered to pay for my educational expenses out of her inheritance, as an investment in me.

Yvonne, I thank you with all of my heart for your sacrifice on my behalf. I also thank your mother who made all of this possible. And finally, I want to thank the *Port O' Call* military ministry for bringing me to Jesus Christ. I will always be humbled and deeply grateful to you all. Thank you.

I also want to express my sincere appreciation to Dr. Al Hill, who served as my field mentor during my doctoral program and as the editor of this book. His assistance and encouragement have been invaluable throughout the process. Thank you, my friend.

Contents

❧❧

Dedication		vii
Chapter 1	**Our Vision—Our Story**	1
Chapter 2	**Why A Specialized Military Ministry?**	13
Chapter 3	**Our Vision**	23
Chapter 4	**Why Hospitality?**	67
Chapter 5	**Making Contact**	83
Chapter 6	**You Invited Me Into Your Lives**	97
Chapter 7	**You Shared Jesus With Me**	123
Chapter 8	**You Shared the Christian Life With Me**	139
Chapter 9	**You Shared the Holy Spirit With Me**	151
Chapter 10	**You Helped Me Share My Faith.**	171
Chapter 11	**You Didn't Forget Me**	185
Chapter 12	**The Continuing Story**	199

1
OUR VISION - OUR STORY

*"Vision is a picture held in your mind's eye
of the way things could or should be in the days ahead."* [1]

❧

This book is about vision—a vision God put in our hearts for ministry to the military. We call it "Pentecostal Hospitality House Military Ministry." It is the picture we hold in our mind's eye of young, single servicemen and women coming to know Jesus Christ as their Savior, and being rooted and grounded in the Word of God. We see them receiving the baptism with the Holy Spirit to divinely empower them to be witnesses for Jesus Christ. And we also see them functioning as culturally sensitive witnesses for Jesus among military personnel in their units, among multinational forces in combined military operations, and among the residents of the countries where they may be sent.

It is also the picture we hold in our mind's eye of faithful Pentecostal people who are involved in good, strong, Pentecostal

---

[1] George Barna, *The Power of Vision: How You Can Capture and Apply God's Vision for your Ministry,* (Ventura, CA: Regal Books, 1992), 29.

churches all over the United States, opening their hearts and homes to young servicemen and women, loving them, and sharing the Full Gospel of Jesus Christ with them.

We see the time when Yvonne and I can say to a young sailor, soldier, marine or airman who has been part of our fellowship and who gets transferred to a military base in another part of the country: "When you get to your new duty station, call Bill and Nancy. They are doing the same thing we are doing here." And we can pick up the phone and call Bill and Nancy and say: "Hey guys, one of our sailors is coming your way. She'll be there next week." Knowing that when she arrives, Bill and Nancy will invite her into their home, love her, build a relationship with her, and help her grow in Christ - or come to know Him.

As we write this book, Yvonne and I have already waited for, worked on and lived this vision for 25 years. We stepped out in faith and followed God's direction. Much of what He promised has been fulfilled; but there is still much that has to *be* fulfilled.

The Port O' Call

Let me back up and share a little bit of our testimony with you.

My story (Yvonne) begins in Castro Valley, California, where I grew up. The foundation of my faith came through a small church that my sister and I attended with our neighbors across the street. As we got older our church attendance stopped, but I never quit believing. Other things occupied my mind: friends, school, etc. But when I went to college I wanted to find a church youth group to participate in for fun. I met a guy in my speech class who invited me to his church and youth group.

Through the kids in that youth group, the pastor's sermons, and the Bible, I learned that Christianity was more than just believing that God and Jesus Christ existed, but that I needed a personal relationship with Jesus Christ.

I remember the Sunday morning on November 10, 1968 when I made my decision to accept Jesus Christ as my Savior. The title of the pastor's sermon was "The Last Call." At the end of the sermon he gave an altar call for anyone who wanted to know Jesus to come forward. My heart was pounding and I was scared to go forward alone. Inside I said, "If someone else goes forward first, then I'll go down." I looked up and someone else was walking to the front. So, I stood up and went forward too.

A woman guided me to a prayer room and talked with me. She said I needed to pray and ask God to forgive my sins, and invite Jesus Christ into my heart. I asked, "Out loud?" She said, "Yes, out loud!" So I did. It was the most wonderful day of my life! I walked all the way home singing the hymn, "*Now I belong to Jesus*." When I got home I shared what happened to me with my mom and dad. And I've never stopped sharing my faith since!

One of my friends was attending The Neighborhood Church in Oakland. It was a church with a burden to reach soldiers, sailors, and marines with the gospel of Jesus Christ. The church provided a home away from home for servicemen in the San Francisco Bay area called The Port O' Call.

The "Port," as we called it for short, conducted Saturday evening evangelistic parties with girls from the church serving as hostesses. There were games and home-cooked meals. And there was even a dormitory if the servicemen wanted to stay over the weekend. Then Sunday afternoon, following the church's worship service, there was another home-cooked meal and softball games. After I accepted Christ as my Savior I started going to the Port with my friend and eventually, became a hostess.

Every Saturday evening, the hostesses (accompanied by some of the guys from the Port who served as hosts) would go into San Francisco and "work the streets." That meant they

You Invited Me In...

would invite servicemen who were on liberty to The Port O' Call for the parties. The sailors who accepted the invitations would get on the "Port Bus" and everyone would ride to Castro Valley together.

I (John) was one of the sailors who accepted that invitation. I was 18-years old. I had been born in Austria and immigrated to the United States with my parents as a little boy. I was raised in Des Moines, Iowa, and grew up attending a Lutheran Church. After graduating from high school I enlisted in the Navy. I went to boot camp in San Diego, California, and was then transferred to Treasure Island for Electronics Technician "A" School.

One Saturday night, I went into San Francisco to find something "fun" to do. A sailor and a young girl came up to me and invited me to a party where they said there would be free food, a place to stay over the weekend, and girls. Right away, I thought, "girls," "free food" and a "place to stay over the weekend." That all sounded like fun (especially the "girls" part) so I accepted their invitation.

I got on the Port Bus and rode for what seemed like an eternity! I had no idea where they were taking us, and it had gotten really dark. We finally arrived, and I noticed a bus stop. So I thought, "Well, at least I could catch a bus back to the base if I needed to." Next to the bus stop there was also a brightly lit marquee that had one large word on it: "FRIENDS." I thought, "Oh no! They're a bunch of Quakers!"

The bus wound its way up a steep curving driveway, through an eight-foot high chain link fence, and around the back of a huge concrete building. It finally came to a stop between two parts of the building and let us off. As soon as we went into the building, I saw a huge picture of Jesus Christ over the fireplace. I had no idea we were going to a Christian party! My first thought was, "Oh no! A bunch of religious fanatics!"

I thought about leaving but hung around for a while to see what would happen. The girls were pretty and friendly, and the games were fun. I was starting to have a fairly good time. So I decided to stay until the party was over. I even stayed overnight in the dormitory to see what the *next* day's activities would be like.

I enjoyed the activities enough that I began attending the parties every weekend. After a few weeks I met Yvonne and asked her for a date. She refused. She explained that she didn't date non-Christians. I argued that I was a Christian! I told her I attended church regularly most of my life, was confirmed when I was 12, and believed all of the major doctrines of the Christian church!

Then she asked me a question I had no answer for: "Do you have a personal relationship with Jesus Christ?" I had no idea what she was talking about.

Then she asked me another question: "Have you ever been born again?" Again, I had no idea what she meant. These were concepts I had never heard before.

She said, "See, you're not a Christian."

Yvonne worked for the Social Security Administration in San Francisco, so several times a week I would drive into the city from Treasure Island, pick her up from work, and give her a ride home to Castro Valley. In rush hour traffic, that was a two-hour trip! While we were in the car we talked and argued about the Bible, about church, about religion, and about faith in Jesus Christ.

I watched the hosts and hostesses at The Port O' Call and could see they were happy. They called themselves Christians, and so did I. But they seemed to have *something* I did not. I didn't know what it was, but I sensed a difference between them and me.

After several weeks of talking with Yvonne, attending the parties, and listening to the director of the center present the gospel, I decided I wanted what they had.

You Invited Me In...

One day, while I was in my barracks room, I prayed, "Lord, if what they are telling me is really true, I want you in my life too. Would you come into my heart, forgive me, and make me the kind of person you want me to be."

Afterward I didn't feel any different, but other sailors I worked with apparently noticed a change in me. They kept asking, "Wagner, what's happened to you?" "What's wrong with you?" I said nothing had happened, but they kept bugging me about it, until I finally asked them what they saw that was different about me. They said, "You don't cuss anymore." I hadn't done that consciously, so I guess God just took it away.

Later, I invited a friend of mine to come to The Port O' Call with me. I told him there were girls, free food, and a place to stay over the weekend. He looked straight at me and asked, "Are you a Christian?"

I had no idea what that had to do with my invitation, but it stopped me. I thought for a second and then said, "Yes...yes I am!" And for the first time, I felt like I really knew what I was talking about. It was actually the first time I confessed my new faith to someone else. And wow! Afterward I had goose bumps from the top of my head to the bottom of my feet! My friend did come to The Port O' Call with me that Saturday night and recommitted his life to Jesus Christ.

From the beginning of my new relationship with Jesus, I wanted to help other sailors come to know Him too. So I approached the man in charge of the prayer room at The Port O' Call and asked if I could work in the prayer room on Saturday nights.

Knowing I was a new Christian, he was surprised by my request and asked, "Are you sure?" I told him I was, and that I wanted to help other sailors accept Christ like I had. He agreed, gave me a small Bible, a gospel tract entitled, "Have You Heard of the Four Spiritual Laws?" and showed me how to help someone who responded to the invitation on Saturday night receive Jesus Christ as their Savior.

Just a little side note: after I accepted Jesus as my Savior, Yvonne and I began "dating." Most of our time together was spent at The Port O' Call. When I finished Electronics "A" school, I got orders to Satellite Communications Class "C" School in Fort Monmouth, New Jersey. But before I left, I asked Yvonne to marry me, and she said "yes"!

Teen Challenge

In 1970, when the movie The Cross and the Switchblade came out, everyone at The Port O' Call went to see it. It was the story of David Wilkerson's ministry among inner city gangs in Brooklyn, New York, and his founding of the Teen Challenge drug rehabilitation program.

When I got to Fort Monmouth in June of 1971, I remembered the movie and decided to go to Brooklyn and visit the Teen Challenge Center there. It was a nice visit, the staff gave me a tour of the facility, and I felt a real love and warmth from the people there.

After I got back to Fort Monmouth, I wanted to find a servicemen's center like The Port O' Call where I could serve the Lord. One particular afternoon, I was driving around Long Branch, New Jersey, and was surprised to see a Teen Challenge center near the base. I thought, "If anyone knew where a servicemen's center was where I could serve the Lord, they would!"

I went in and asked if anyone there knew where a servicemen's center was. The director was out, so I was told to come back the following day, which I did. I asked the director if he knew of any servicemen's centers in the area where I could serve the Lord. He said he did not, but that I was welcome to serve the Lord at his center.

He asked me two questions that reminded me a lot of my original conversation with Yvonne. He asked, "Do you know Jesus Christ as your personal Savior?" To which I responded immediately and with assurance, "Yes, I do!" Then he asked me how I felt about speaking in tongues. Again, as with Yvonne's questions, I had no answers. I said, "I've never heard about speaking in tongues. If it's from God I want it, but if it's not, I don't." That was good enough for him, and he welcomed me into his ministry.

I began driving the center van, praying with drug addicts going through withdrawal, and leading devotions for the residents during chapel services. This was also the first place I witnessed a miracle. I was asked to sit through the night with one of the new residents in the program who would be going through withdrawal during the night. I sat and prayed for this man throughout the night. It was really boring. Nothing happened and he slept through the night peacefully.

But in the morning, when he woke up, he told me I had witnessed a miracle. He explained that of the many times he had gone through withdrawal he never had one like that night. His withdrawals were always violent, with lots of painful cramping, convulsions and vomiting! He had never slept through the night like that with absolutely no symptoms.

It was during this time that all the residents visited an Assemblies of God church that was in the midst of a powerful revival. It was at the height of the Jesus Movement and many young people were getting saved. The church was packed out!

The pastor was preaching about the baptism with the Holy Spirit. And during two different services, I responded by going forward during his altar call for prayer to receive the baptism with the Holy Spirit. I didn't receive it either time and was really embarrassed. So I decided not to respond that way anymore.

Instead, I began asking God to baptize me with the Holy Spirit in my personal daily devotional times. I asked God not to let me make up something out of my own imagination, or simply imitate others, or, worst of all, receive something counterfeit from Satan.

After several weeks of praying and asking God to baptize me with the Holy Spirit, a short phrase that sounded a lot like gibberish, went through my mind. I dismissed it because everyone else I had ever heard speak in tongues spoke in what seemed like long, flowing sentences.

But, every time I asked God to baptize me with the Holy Spirit, nothing but the same little phrase went through my mind. I finally quit asking.

Eula ("Sister") Robinson

In January of 1972, after graduating from "C" school, I was transferred to Naval Communications Station Honolulu, in Hawaii. One of the hosts at The Port O' Call recommended I visit Kapahulu Bible Church in Honolulu, which I did. There I met Eula Robinson, a 60-year old widow from Birmingham, Alabama. A petite little woman, with snow white coiffured hair and a pleasant southern accent. "Sister Robinson" (as we called her), was a missionary in Hawaii who ministered to servicemen in her home. She invited soldiers, sailors, and marines to her home after church for a home-cooked meal on Sundays, and for fellowship and prayer during the week.

She lived in Wahiawa, and that Sunday invited me to her home for dinner after church. Since Wahiawa was close to the base where I was stationed, I accepted her invitation. When I got to her apartment I met other sailors and a soldier who were part of her fellowship. She was a good cook!

I enjoyed her hospitality and the fellowship, so I spent a lot of time in her home. She didn't drive, and I had a car, so all of us did a lot of sightseeing around the island on my days off. That created a lot of really neat memories.

As I got to know her, I came to think of her as having a "red phone" that was a direct line to God. She was so demure and quiet, yet it seemed whenever she prayed God answered! She became a spiritual mentor for me. The way she focused on the Word of God and prayer was inspiring, and really helped me grow in my new faith.

As I mentioned, I was introduced to the baptism with the Holy Spirit while I was stationed in New Jersey, but never actually experienced it for myself. One summer, Sister Robinson had two friends from the mainland visiting her. We went sightseeing around the island with them, and that evening after dinner, joined together for prayer.

While we were praying, one of her friends began praying in tongues. I was familiar with the sound of people doing that, but her praying sounded unusual. She seemed to simply repeat one little phrase over and over again. I turned to her and quietly, but rather abruptly asked, "Is that all you pray in tongues?"

She was startled by my question, but responded very kindly, "Yes, that's all the Lord has ever given me. Why?"

I explained, "I've been praying to receive the baptism with the Holy Spirit for several months. But whenever I pray, the only thing that comes to my mind is a very short little phrase similar to yours. I always thought that couldn't be right because it was too short. Whenever I heard other people pray in tongues their language always seemed long and flowing."

She smiled and gently said, "Use whatever the Lord gives you. And if He wants you to have more He will give you more."

I thanked her, and we went back to prayer. I felt a tightness in my chest after that, like something wanted to come out, or like there was something I really needed to say. But I couldn't bring myself to do it. Eventually the prayer meeting ended, and I went back to the base.

When I got to the barracks, just as I crossed the threshold of my room, another short phrase in tongues came to my mind. This one was a little longer than the ones I had experienced before.

Suddenly, I felt like the Lord spoke to me and said, "Say it."

I said, "I can't."

He said, "Why? No one is here. Your roommates are all gone. No one will hear you."

But again, I said, "I can't."

With more insistence the Lord said, "Say it!"

So I whispered it under my breath. At that, He said more forcefully, "I SAID, SAY IT OUT LOUD!"

So I did. And as soon as I said the phrase out loud I knew I had received the baptism with the Holy Spirit!

I was so excited I ran down three flights of stairs to call Yvonne (who was in California) to let her know. It was midnight in Hawaii and I forgot about the three-hour time difference between Hawaii and the mainland. I woke her up at three in the morning!

She was still not sure about the whole "speaking in tongues" thing, and actually had her church praying for me, thinking I had gone off the deep end. So her reception on the phone was less than enthusiastic!

So I called Sister Robinson to tell her. When she answered the phone, I realized I had awakened her out of a sound sleep, too. Excitedly, I said, "I got it!" She chuckled and said quietly, "I knew you would."

The next day we went sightseeing again and I kept repeating the phrase to myself over and over so I wouldn't forget it. I didn't forget it, and sometime later, the Lord did give me more.

In September, I went home on leave. Yvonne and I got married, and she joined me at Sister Robinson's fellowship. The first month we lived in the Guest House on Schofield Barracks. While we were there, kneeling next to our bed, Yvonne received the baptism with the Holy Spirit and spoke in tongues!

2

WHY A SPECIAL MINISTRY TO THE MILITARY?

Now that you know a little about our personal and spiritual backgrounds, let me fast forward to today. Yvonne and I have been engaged in military ministry for decades. The last 18 years have found us working in the military "hub" of the Norfolk-Virginia Beach area.

Prior to moving here, we spent 20 years in the United States Navy. In addition to serving ten years as an enlisted electronics technician, I served ten years as a Navy chaplain. There are many things I saw and learned during that time about life in the military, and what young servicemen and women go through. Most people who have never served in the military have no experience nor understand what these young people deal with on a daily basis. Many in our society, including some of those who are new to military life, think being in the military is just like any other job. But it is not!

The military is unique. It is, first and foremost, a war-fighting institution with its own language, values, customs, and culture. In addition, for national security reasons, the military also maintains very restricted access to its installations, effectively creating a barrier between the military community and the surrounding civilian population. All of this creates a civilization within a civilization.

The vast majority of those serving in the military are young adults between the ages of 18 and 25. Young men and women who, when they entered the military, may have been flipping burgers at McDonald's or bagging groceries at the local supermarket. These young people quickly become highly trained and motivated warriors, holding amazingly powerful weapons in their hands.

The military strives to instill character traits such as duty, honor, country, courage and commitment in these young warriors. It trains them to live in an authoritarian environment where immediate and unquestioned obedience to commands is demanded and enforced. It severely restructures their lives, and even restricts and controls their free time. This forced regimentation often comes as a shock to a new enlistee, who as a teenager may have just started asserting his or her independence from mom and dad.

Add to this the fact that, for the first time in their lives, many of them are geographically removed from the influence of their family and friends and everything familiar to them. They now have large amounts of discretionary spending money, and are surrounded by other young men and women from a variety of cultural backgrounds. With this diminished family influence, their new found financial freedom and increased peer pressure, a significant number of these young adults begin making poor personal choices: turning to alcohol, drugs, and sexual activity to entertain or console themselves.

It is also not unusual for *Christian* young people entering the military to feel like they are the only Christian in their unit. So without adequate spiritual support or fellowship (and feeling peer pressure from new friends who do not share their faith),

Why a Special Ministry to the Military?

they can drift away from the church, from their spiritual roots and even from their faith in Jesus Christ.

For many young people, joining the military was supposed to be an exciting adventure. It was advertised as an opportunity to "see the world" and "be all you can be." They may even have accepted the idea that joining the military was a quick and easy way to pay for a college education.

But for most of them, the reality turns out to be another thing entirely! They experience long, grueling, 12- to 18-hour work days, followed by additional hours of watch standing, studying for promotion exams and what seems like endless mundane "cleaning" details. For many, something as basic as *sleep* becomes a prized and precious commodity.

Aboard Navy ships, for example, a sailor's life literally involves eating, sleeping, working and playing on a floating factory, for weeks and months at a time. Sailors with families have to cope with long and often unexpected periods of separation. And in the midst of all this busyness and pressure, they also have to deal with extended periods of inactivity and boredom.

Because the military is first and foremost a war-fighting institution, the greatest stressor that members of the armed forces have to face is the heightened possibility of death itself. As these young warriors enter combat, or even routine operational situations, they have to deal with the potential of being killed, watching a friend die or having to kill another human being in the line of duty.

All of these dynamics impact young servicemen and women. Many get overwhelmed morally, spiritually, emotionally, and psychologically. An ever increasing number become so despondent that they lose hope, and feel so helpless they consider, attempt, and even commit suicide. Statistically, suicide has been on the rise in the military for years.[2] Some even consider the suicide rate in the military to be "epidemic," especially in the Army. In an article published in the American Journal of Public Health entitled, *Suicide Incidence and Risk Factors in an Active Duty US Military Population* Jeffrey Hyman noted that, "The suicide rate increased for all services between 2005 and 2007. The increase was greatest for the Regular Army and National Guard."[3]

The Department of Defense recognizes the magnitude of the pressures placed on the young men and women it enlists, and conducts a survey of the health of the active duty military community every three years. The DoD Survey of Health Related Behaviors[4] has been the main source of health behavior information for the military since 1980. The statistics from these studies are published in the *Survey of Health Related Behaviors Among Military Personnel*[5] with the conclusions and recommendations being used to determine human resource management decisions that affect the overall health and welfare of the military community.

In 2005, the category of "religiosity/spirituality" was included in the Department of Defense survey. Researchers found that "20% of military personnel were categorized as

---

[2] Gregg Zoroya. "U.S. Military Suicides Remain High For 7th Year." *USA Today*. Updated May 4, 2016. https://www.usatoday.com/story/news/nation/2016/04/01/us-military-suicides-remain-stubbornly-high/82518278/.
[3] Jeffrey Hyman, Robert Ireland, Lucinda Frost, Linda Cottrell. "Suicide Incidence and Risk Factors in an Active Duty US Military Population." *Am J Public Health*. 2012 Mar; 102(Suppl 1): S138–S146. Published online 2012 Mar. doi: 10.2105/AJPH.2011.300484 PMCID: PMC3496445.
[4] Military Health System. "Survey of Health Related Behaviors." https://health.mil/Military-Health-Topics/Access-Cost-Quality-and-Safety/Health-Care-Program-Evaluation/Survey-of-Health-Related-Behaviors.
[5] 2011 Department of Defense Health Related Behaviors Survey of Active Duty Military Personnel, https://www.murray.senate.gov/public/_cache/files/889efd07-2475-40ee-b3b0-508947957a0f/final-2011-hrb-active-duty-survey-report.pdf, 1.

having high religiosity/spirituality. More than half were categorized as having a medium level, and almost one-fourth were categorized as having low religiosity/spirituality."[6] In this survey researchers commented that some statistically significant differences between spirituality levels were noted when considering selected health and stress measures. They went on:

> For instance, persons categorized as being highly religious/spiritual were less likely to be heavy alcohol users, cigarette smokers, or illicit drug users. They were also less likely to engage in risky behaviors, to meet criteria for need of further evaluation for depression or anxiety, perceive "a lot" of stress at work or in their family, or indicate they had seriously considered suicide in the year prior to the survey than those categorized as having a low level of religiosity/spirituality.[7]

While this "religiosity/spirituality" category was not specifically "Christian" in perspective, it is not difficult to reason from the evidence that helping military men and women begin and develop a personal relationship with Jesus Christ can significantly improve their lives in the military, and help them deal with the stress factors associated with military life.

As highly trained and motivated as these young warriors are for combat, Yvonne and I believe they must also be *spiritually* prepared for combat. They have to understand the very real possibility that if they are called upon to make the supreme sacrifice on the battlefield, they will also have to face Jesus Christ as their eternal judge. The most important question every young military man and woman must answer, and one they may not even be asking, is: "If I were to die suddenly in combat, where would I spend eternity?"

---

[6] Robert M. Bray, 2005 Department of Defense Survey of Health Related Behaviors Among Military Personnel, 2005, 239.
[7] Ibid.

Young men and women who enter the military need to establish a personal relationship with Jesus Christ *before* they go into combat. Their relationship with Him must to be strong enough to sustain them on the battlefield. And, it must be strong enough to sustain them when they come home. They need to be grounded and established in their understanding of the biblical concept of forgiveness through Jesus Christ and His sacrifice on the cross. Only by having personally understood and experienced Jesus' forgiveness will they be able to forgive themselves, and live with the memories, of some of the actions they may have had to take on the battlefield. The sights, sounds, and smells of war can impact and devastate a young person's life emotionally, mentally, physically, and spiritually long after they leave the battlefield.

Unfortunately, the statistics for this age group's interest in spiritual things is not encouraging. David Kinnaman and Thom Rainer both write about surveys they conducted of Millennials (young adults between the ages of 18 and 30). Kinnaman observes that "the ages eighteen to twenty-nine are the black hole of church attendance; this age segment is 'missing in action' from most congregations."[8] He goes on to note that "there is a 43 percent drop-off between the teen and early adult years in terms of church engagement."[9] Thom and Jess Rainer observed in their studies that, "Overall, spiritual matters were unimportant to these young adults. Only 13 percent of them viewed religion and spiritual matters with any degree of importance."[10] Said another way, 87 percent of those in this age group view God, religion, and spiritual matters as irrelevant to their lives!

---

[8] David Kinnaman, *You Lost Me: Why Young Christians Are Leaving Church...And Rethinking Faith* (Grand Rapids: Baker Books, 2011), 22.
[9] Ibid.
[10] Thom S Rainer and Jess W. Rainer, *The Millennials: Connecting to America's Largest Generation* (Nashville: B&H Publishing Co.), 111.

So why do I share this statistic with you, and why is it important in relation to military ministry? Because, as I mentioned earlier, the vast majority of people serving in the United States military are between the ages of 18 and 25, and most of them have never been born again. They do not have a personal relationship with Jesus Christ; and what's worse, they may not even care!

Military Ministry and Civilian Young Adult Ministry

Some people ask us what the difference is between ministering to military young adults and civilian young adults. They often ask, "Why not simply include military young adults in a church's civilian young adult ministry? After all, they are the same age."

While it is true they are the same age *chronologically*, because of their stage in life, ministering to young men and women in the military is significantly different than ministering to civilian young people despite this similarity of age.

For example, civilian young adults are usually in their home town, in their home church, and near their biological families and lifelong friends. Young adults serving in the armed forces on the other hand, are usually in a strange city, away from their home church, and away from their families and friends. As a result, they are often homesick and lonely, looking for acceptance, friendship and somewhere to belong.

Because civilian young adults already have their circle of family and friends nearby, they may not feel the need, nor have the desire, to welcome a serviceman or woman who visits their church into their inner circle of friends.

Another significant difference between the civilian and military young adult is in the relative permanence and stability of the civilian young adult's life, as compared to the transience and instability of the young military person's life. Civilian young adults who live in military communities are keenly aware of the transience of military personnel. And, because they know the young military person will repeatedly leave the area, and will eventually be transferred away permanently, there is often a reluctance to reach out to establish friendships with him or her.

Similarly, because a young serviceman's training, and the focus of his or her daily life, revolves around military specific activities, their interests and the things they talk about will be related to the military and their military jobs. The civilian young adult often knows nothing about these activities and may have no interest in them.

While servicemen and women travel to many strange and exotic places in the world, civilian young adults may not have traveled extensively, and may not understand or be interested in the service member's military travels or experiences. Likewise, the things a civilian young adult is interested in may not interest the young military man and woman—or may remind him or her of home and what they left behind, making their loneliness all the more painful.

Sometimes a soldier or marine will go into a combat situation in a time of war. And for national security reasons, he may not be able to talk about where he's been or what he did. This secrecy can be perceived as aloofness by the civilian young adult and add to the distance and difference between the two groups.

So while military and civilian young adults may be the same age, and therefore seem as though they should have everything in common, the differences between the two groups are significant, and can often be intensely felt by both. The feeling of being unwelcome or an outsider often causes the young military person to stay away from local churches.

These differences in the life situations of young servicemen and women and civilian young adults are the very factors that make hospitality house military ministry so important and necessary. This specialized ministry targets the specific needs of

Why a Special Ministry to the Military?

the serviceman and woman, and takes the military's transient nature into account.

God's Call to Open Our Home

In June of 2000, the Lord called Yvonne and me to a new season of ministry, and brought us to Virginia Beach to reach young single servicemen and women for Jesus Christ. We originally thought we would pattern our ministry after The Port O' Call in California, with a building, hosts and hostesses, and a ministry large enough to reach many of the thousands of servicemen and women stationed in this area.

But one day while I was praying about where to look for a building, God spoke to my heart and said, "I don't want you to look for a building; I want you to minister in your home."

I was surprised and asked, "Why, Lord? We could get so many more people into a different building. We can only fit about 20 people, at the most, into our home!"

He said: "I know, but the young people in the military today are different than you were 30 years ago. When you were 18, you came from an intact family, you had a church background, and you believed in God and the Bible. Most of the young people in the military today that you will be ministering to will come from broken or dysfunctional families, little (if any) church background and little or no belief in God or the Bible. Servicemen and women today need a loving family environment where they can see Christ's love lived out in front of them. They need to be loved into the kingdom."

I knew from that moment we would open our home and invite them in. And that is what Yvonne and I have been doing every weekend for 18 years. *You Invited Me In...* is our story: ours, and that of the young servicemen and women who have been through our home and become part of our extended family.

3

OUR VISION

In this chapter, I want to share the *details* of the vision God put in our hearts for Pentecostal hospitality house military ministry. As I begin, let me recall the comment by George Barna about vision that opened Chapter 1 where he said: "Vision is a picture held in your mind's eye of the way things could or should be in the future."[11]

As I mentioned in Chapter 1, this vision has two very distinct parts and comes out of my devotional time spent in the Word of God and prayer in 1993. The first part is the picture of young, single servicemen and women coming to know Jesus Christ as their Savior and being rooted and grounded in the Word of God. Then receiving the baptism with the Holy Spirit and becoming culturally sensitive witnesses for Jesus Christ. A picture that is based on Isaiah 43 verses 5 and 6:

Do not be afraid, for I am with you;
  I will bring your children from the east
and gather you from the west.
  I will say to the north, 'Give them up!'

---

[11] See the footnote on page 1.

> *and to the south, 'Do not hold them back.'*
>   *Bring my sons from afar*
> *and my daughters from the ends of the earth....*

The second part is the picture of Pentecostal people all over the United States who live near military bases, involved in good strong Pentecostal churches, opening their hearts and homes to young, single, servicemen and women, and sharing the Full Gospel with them. A picture that is based on Isaiah 51 verses 1 and 2:

> *Listen to me, you who pursue righteousness*
>   *And who seek the Lord:*
> *Look to the rock from which you were cut*
>   *and to the quarry from which you were hewn;*
> *look to Abraham, your father,*
>   *and to Sarah, who gave you birth.*
> *When I called him he was only one man,*
>   *and I blessed him and made him many.*

Writing the Vision and Making it Plain

So, why am I sharing this vision and making it public? Because I believe God told me to. Through Habakkuk 2:2, the Lord said I was to write the vision and make it plain, so that those who read it could run with it. Our hope is that, after reading our vision you will be encouraged and motivated to get involved in Pentecostal hospitality house military ministry.

In Habakkuk 2:3, the Lord assured us that the vision would surely be fulfilled at an appointed time. But even if that time were delayed, we were to wait for it, because the vision would not fail. As I write this chapter, Yvonne and I have already worked and waited for the fulfillment of this vision for 25 years. In June of 2000 we stepped out in faith and followed God's direction and moved to Virginia Beach. Over the course of the last 18 years much of what He promised has been fulfilled, yet

Our Vision

there is still much to be fulfilled. The rest of this chapter contains the details of this vision and the scriptures those details are based on. In later chapters I will share the specifics of how God has been fulfilling this vision and continues to do so.

The Beginning

Let me go back to the beginning of the story. In 1987, I was back in the Navy on active duty a second time, serving as a chaplain. The Navy had sent me (with my wife and two young daughters) back to Hawaii. Then in 1990, I was diagnosed with a medical condition that, if not corrected, could have left me a quadriplegic by my mid-fifties. My family and I were flown to Oakland, California, where they operated on my spinal cord. The surgery was successful, but the underlying condition resulted in my being medically retired from the Navy. At that point I really didn't know what the future would hold.

On our way out of the hospital, Yvonne suggested we stop in the gift shop. There, printed on a piece of paper taped to the wall behind the cashier, was Jeremiah 29:11: *"For I know the plans I have for you," declares the Lord, "plans to prosper you and not to harm you, plans to give you hope and a future."* That verse gave me the assurance that God knew where I was, what I had been through, and that He still had a plan for my life!

After my retirement from the Navy, we moved to Grand Junction, Colorado to plant a church. Our daughters remembered the description of our activities at The Port O' Call, and suggested we pattern our church-planting efforts after those activities. Their idea was to invite some of their high school friends to our home one afternoon a week to eat, play games, and have a short Bible study. Yvonne and I thought that was a great idea!

The effort was a great success, and from 1990 to 1993, we ministered to over 200 teenagers in our home. Every Thursday afternoon we had as many as 25 high school students in our living room. Some of them even told their parents they were "going to church" when they came over to the house. Eight of the teens and one parent accepted Jesus Christ as their Savior and were baptized in water. It was an exciting time! But as with so many things in life, there was a time and season for that outreach. Gradually, the young people who came to the house got involved in other activities, graduated from high school, and went on to colleges and careers.

So our ministry changed again, and I began traveling as an itinerant personal evangelist to various towns in the deserts of western Colorado, Wyoming, Utah, New Mexico, and Arizona. There I would witness to people I met about Jesus Christ. On the weekends Yvonne and I would visit churches in those towns to introduce ourselves to the local pastors, and establish relationships with them, in order to recommend their churches to the people we witnessed to.

It was during this time that I read through Isaiah and Jeremiah in my daily devotions. From June to November of 1993 the Lord began speaking to my heart through those two books of the Bible about the future of our ministry, and this vision was born. However, it was another seven years before God brought us to Virginia, and showed us that the vision applied to ministry among young servicemen and women.

The Call of God

I believe God has specific plans for everyone's lives. While most of the events in the early, formative years of childhood often seem random and arbitrary, God is in control of them all, including where and when a person is born. Acts 17:26 says:

From one man he made all the people of the world. Now they live all over the earth. He decided exactly when they should live. And he decided exactly where they should live.[12]

By faith, we believe God determined those things for Yvonne and me. Let me explain what I mean.

My (John) father was a German, born in Yugoslavia, in 1928. Following World War II, at the age of 19, he fled the country because of the oppressive regime of Josip Tito. He became a refugee in Austria where he met and married my mother.

In 1951, in Linz, Austria, my twin sister and I were born. Both of us had life-threatening stomach disorders and neither of us were expected to live. I did; my sister did not. Then when I was four years old, my family emigrated from Austria to the United States and settled in Des Moines, Iowa where I grew up.

As a child, all of these events were totally out of my control. After I became an adult I often felt conflicted about having lost my twin sister, my extended family, my native country and language. So I was really encouraged when the Lord spoke to me through Jeremiah 1:5, and said,

Before I formed you in the womb I knew you,
  before you were born I set you apart;
I appointed you as a prophet to the nations.

In three other passages God showed me that He knew exactly where I came from and where I was living. In Isaiah 41 verse 2 He asked me a question, and then answered it in verse 4:

Who stirred up one from the east,
  calling him in righteousness to His service?

---

[12] (NIRV), New International Readers Version.

You Invited Me In...

> *I, the Lord—with the first of them*
> *and with the last—I am he.*

In verses 9 and 10 He said,

> *I took you from the ends of the earth;*
> *from its farthest corners I called you.*
> *I said, 'You are my servant';*
> *I have chosen you and have not rejected you.*
> *So do not fear, for I am with you;*
> *do not be dismayed, for I am your God.*
> *I will strengthen you and help you;*
> *I will uphold you with my righteous right hand.*

And finally, in Isaiah 46:11, He said,

> *From the east I summon a bird of prey;*
> *from a far-off land, a man to fulfill my purpose.*

As I read those passages I thought, "I'm from Austria. Austria is a far-off land and east of the United States!" God knew exactly when and where I was born. And not only did He know where I grew up, He knew, as a child, all of the things I would leave behind. All because of the purpose He had for my life before I was even born.

My (Yvonne) mother was born in Germany in 1910. And in 1935 emigrated from Germany to the United States to escape the oppression of the Hitler regime. Settling in San Francisco, she eventually met and married my dad. And in 1950 moved to Castro Valley, CA. where I was born and grew up.

None of the early events of our lives were accidental or merely coincidental. They were all divinely planned by God, who brought me from Austria to Des Moines, Iowa and then to

Castro Valley. He also brought Yvonne's mother from Germany to Castro Valley, and there brought Yvonne and me together.

Preparation for Ministry

God not only called us, but prepared us for this ministry as well. In Isaiah 50, verses 4 and 5, He said,

The Sovereign Lord has given me a well-instructed tongue,
  to know the word that sustains the weary.
He wakens me morning by morning,
  wakens my ear to listen like one being instructed.
The Sovereign Lord has opened my ears;
  I have not been rebellious,
I have not turned away.

God's preparation of us for this ministry was educational, experiential, and spiritual. In the first year of my life as a Christian, God gave me the desire to help other sailors come to know Jesus Christ as their Savior. He provided the training for me to do that through the prayer room ministry at The Port O' Call. And not long afterward, provided a training opportunity for both Yvonne and me through the Campus Crusade for Christ Lay Institute for Evangelism, to learn how to do personal evangelism using the *Have You Heard of the Four Spiritual Laws* gospel tract.

When my initial enlistment in the Navy ended, I went on to Bible College and seminary to acquire the educational skills necessary to do the work God had for me to do. I earned the Bachelor of Arts Degree in Bible from Central Bible College, and the Master of Divinity Degree from the Assemblies of God Theological Seminary in Springfield, Missouri.

After moving to Virginia Beach, I continued my studies and earned the Doctor of Ministry degree at Regent University. There I completed a ministry project that involved an in-depth evaluation of the first seven years of our military ministry here. My studies culminated with the writing of a dissertation as a case study and model for Pentecostal hospitality house military ministry.

Yvonne and I believe that every part of our ministry prior to coming to Virginia was in preparation for this work. God never wastes our life experiences, but uses them as training for what lies ahead. God's preparation of us included 28 years of ministerial experience. In Isaiah 55:4, He said,

See, I have made him a witness to the peoples,
a ruler and commander of the peoples.

That "making" included our time as a host and hostess at The Port O' Call. And it included my volunteer work as a live-in counselor at the Long Branch Teen Challenge Center while I was stationed in New Jersey.

After Yvonne and I were married, it included our ministry directing the National Correspondence Institute in Hawaii. It also included my service as a Navy chaplain in Missouri, Maine and Hawaii. The churches we planted in Maine and Colorado, and our ministry as itinerant personal evangelists in six western states were all part of our ministry experiences preparing us for our ministry in Virginia.

Then there was also the spiritual preparation for this ministry. God called it a "refining" process that included some significant trials and difficulties over the years. In Isaiah 48, verses 10 and 11, the Lord said:

See, I have refined you, though not as silver;
  I have tested you in the furnace of affliction.
For my own sake, for my own sake, I do this.
  How can I let myself be defamed?
I will not yield my glory to another.

Our Vision

The trials we went through in our lives were meant to draw us closer to the Lord and teach us to draw our strength from Him. They were also meant to teach us to always give Him the credit and glory for everything we accomplished, including all of the results in our ministry.

During my Christian life, I often prayed that God would make my ministry just like Jesus' ministry. So I knew He was answering my prayers when in Isaiah 42, verses 6 and 7, He said,

I, the Lord, have called you in righteousness;
I will take hold of your hand.
I will keep you and will make you
to be a covenant for the people
and a light for the Gentiles,
to open eyes that are blind,
to free captives from prison
and to release from the dungeon those who sit in
darkness.

One of my favorite passages of scripture has always been 2 Timothy 2:21, where God talks about being an instrument for noble purposes, useful to God, and prepared for His service. I've always wanted to be that kind of an instrument, so I took to heart the word the Lord spoke to me in Isaiah 49, verses 2 and 3, where using a double metaphor, He said:

He made my mouth like a sharpened sword,
in the shadow of his hand he hid me;
he made me into a polished arrow
and concealed me in his quiver.
He said to me, "You are my servant,
...in whom I will display my splendor.

You Invited Me In...

When God first gave me this vision, I knew the work He had for us was still in the future. And as a warrior conceals his sword in his hand until it is needed in battle—and an archer keeps his arrows in their quiver until they are needed to shoot at a target—I knew the Lord would use us when He was ready.

God's Plans

God told us He knew the plans He had for us. They were plans to prosper us and not to harm us. And, they were plans meant to give us hope and a future. When God first began laying out His vision for this ministry in 1993, He said, through Isaiah 46:8-11:

Remember this, keep it in mind...
I am God, and there is no other;
I am God, and there is none like me.
I make known the end from the beginning,
from ancient times, what is still to come.
I say, 'My purpose will stand,
and I will do all that I please.'...
What I have said, that I will bring about;
what I have planned, that I will do.

He was telling us that this vision was *His* plan, and He was revealing it to us ahead of time. He was also promising to actually bring His plans to fruition! In Isaiah 55, verses 10 and 11, the Lord again said His word and this vision would be fulfilled:

As the rain and the snow
  come down from heaven,
and do not return to it
  without watering the earth
and making it bud and flourish,

*so that it yields seed for the sower and bread for the
    eater,
so is my word that goes out from my mouth:
    It will not return to me empty,
but will accomplish what I desire
    and achieve the purpose for which I sent it.*

I needed these repeated promises and assurances from God, because when He first began revealing this vision to me I was overwhelmed! What God was saying in this vision was far more than we could accomplish on our own. It was far greater than I could even believe for at the time. I felt much like the prophet in Jeremiah 1:6, when he said:

Alas, Sovereign Lord…I do not know how to speak; I am too young.

But as with the prophet, the Lord said to me in verse 7:

Do not say, 'I'm too young.' You must go to everyone I send you to. You must say everything I command you to say.

And then in verse 10 the Lord said:

I have put my words in your mouth. Today I am appointing you to speak to nations and kingdoms.

God clearly had a work for us to do. In the midst of God speaking to Jeremiah, in verse 11, He showed the prophet the branch of a tree and asked him what he saw. Jeremiah replied that he saw the branch of an almond tree. To which God replied in verse 12:

You Invited Me In...

> *You have seen correctly. I am watching to see that my word comes true.*

God's word to us was that He was watching to see that His word would come true in our lives as well. Now, 18 years after coming to Virginia Beach, we can look back and see that many of the promises God made to us have come to pass. And the parts that have been fulfilled help us believe that the rest will be fulfilled as well.

God Declares New Things

As God continued to reveal His vision to us He said in Isaiah 42:9 that He was going to do "new things."

> *What I said would happen has taken place.*
>   *Now I announce new things to you.*
> *Before they even begin to happen,*
>   *I announce them to you.*

And in Isaiah 43:18-19, He said,

> Forget the things that happened in the past.
>   Do not keep on thinking about them.
> I am about to do something new.
>   It is beginning to happen even now.
>   Don't you see it coming?

While there was nothing wrong with what we had done in the past, God was telling us that He wanted us to focus on the future, on the new things He was about to bring into existence.

As I read Isaiah 42:9-12, I was surprised just how specifically God knew the "former" things we had done. He even mentioned the exact areas of ministry Yvonne and I had been involved in. In verse 10, He said,

Our Vision

> *Sing to the Lord a new song,*
> *Sing His praise from the end of the earth!*
> *You who go down to the sea, and all that is in it...* [13]

As an Electronics Technician in the Navy, I served aboard ships at sea. And as a Navy Chaplain, I went down *into* the sea and ministered to sailors on submarines.

In verse 11, God said,

Let the desert and its towns raise their voices... [14]

At the time God gave me this vision, Yvonne and I were ministering in Grand Junction, Colorado, and several small towns in six surrounding states. All of them were in the desert of the western United States.

Finally, in verse 12, God said,

Let them give glory to the Lord
  and proclaim His praise in the islands.

When Yvonne and I were first married, we served the Lord together in Hawaii. I was stationed there as an electronics technician and during my off-duty hours, I served as the director of the National Correspondence Institute, an evangelistic ministry of the Assemblies of God.

Our pastor brought the NCI program into our church as a way of following up visitors and new converts. The work developed into a state-wide ministry in which evangelistic Bible study courses were mailed throughout the Hawaiian Islands. People from every island accepted Jesus Christ as their Savior

---

[13] (NASB), New American Standard Bible.
[14] (NIRV), New International Readers Version.

through these courses. We also sent them into the Honolulu State Prison where inmates accepted Christ as their Savior. Our ministry slogan was *"Declaring His Praise in the Islands."*

So God showed me that He knew exactly where we had ministered and what we had done. But now He was telling us it was time for new beginnings, and new things to come into existence. Our thoughts were not to be focused on memories of the past, but on the vision of things God was planning for the future.

The Lord's instructions to us were clear when He said, through Isaiah 54:2-4,

Enlarge the place of your tent,
 stretch your tent curtains wide,
do not hold back;
 lengthen your cords,
strengthen your stakes.
 For you will spread out to the right and to the left...

Wanting us to move forward with confidence, He added a word of encouragement at the end of verse 4:

Do not be afraid; you will not be put to shame.
 Do not fear disgrace; you will not be humiliated.

Not long after moving to Virginia, I was praying and reading through the book of Haggai. And again the Lord spoke about our past ministry. In Chapter 1, verses 5 and 7, He said twice that we were to give careful thought to our ways.

And in Chapter 2, verses 4 through 9, He said we were to think carefully about what we were doing in this new work; we were to be strong and *do* the work, promising:

Our Vision

For I am with you declares the Lord Almighty. This is what I covenanted with you when you came out of Egypt. And my Spirit remains among you. Do not fear.[15]

We were to be strong, moving forward with confidence, knowing that God Himself would be with us, and that the Holy Spirit would remain among us. We were not to be afraid. We did not literally come out of Egypt, but God *had* covenanted with us concerning this ministry when He brought us out of Grand Junction and to Virginia Beach.

God said He would guide us clearly in the days ahead. Even though we would be traveling along an unfamiliar path, and a way we had never traveled before. In Isaiah 42:16, He said,

I will lead the blind by ways they have not known,
  along unfamiliar paths I will guide them;
I will turn the darkness into light before them
  and make the rough places smooth.
These are the things I will do;
  I will not forsake them.

He has been with us, and has guided us in this ministry for 18 years! He has never forsaken us!

I also read through the book of Micah, where the Lord gave me the scope of this vision and our future ministry. In Micah 7:11-12, He said,

The day for building your walls will come,
  the day for extending your boundaries.
In that day people will come to you...
  from sea to sea
and from mountain to mountain.

---

[15] Haggai 2:4-5.

You Invited Me In...

And in Isaiah 49:6, He said,

> *I will also make you a light for the Gentiles,
> that you may bring my salvation to the ends of the earth.*

Through these verses God said our ministry would have a national *and* global impact. We would reach people from coast to coast in the United States, as well as around the world, bringing them the message of salvation in Jesus Christ.

In Haggai 2, verses 7 and 9, the Lord said,

> *...I will fill this house with glory, says the Lord Almighty....The glory of the present house will be greater than the glory of the former house, says the Lord Almighty. And in this place I will grant peace, declares the Lord Almighty.*

God knew what we had done in our home in Colorado, ministering to high school students. In this verse, He was telling us that our ministry with young military men and women in our home in Virginia, would be greater than what we had done in Colorado.

He promised to grant peace to those who would came into our home in Virginia Beach, just as He had granted peace to the teens who came into our home in Grand Junction.

Salvation

The Lord repeated several times that His purpose for this ministry was the salvation of young servicemen and women. In Isaiah 51:5, He said,

> *My righteousness draws near speedily,
> my salvation is on the way...*

Our Vision

And in Isaiah 41:17-20 He showed us that He sees the spiritual condition of these young people:

> *The poor and needy search for water,*
>   *but there is none;*
>   *their tongues are parched with thirst.*
> *But I the Lord will answer them;*
>   *I, the God of Israel, will not forsake them.*
> *I will make rivers flow on barren heights,*
>   *and springs within the valleys.*
> *I will turn the desert into pools of water,*
>   *and the parched ground into springs.*
> *I will put in the desert*
>   *the cedar and the acacia, the myrtle and the olive.*
> *I will set junipers in the wasteland,*
>   *the fir and the cypress together,*
> *so that people may see and know,*
>   *may consider and understand,*
> *that the hand of the Lord has done this,*
>   *that the Holy One of Israel has created it.*

In the application of this passage to our context of ministry, God was saying that it is the young military men and women who are spiritually poor and needy. They search for "water," but there is none. Their tongues are parched with thirst. Unfortunately, many of them don't even realize they are thirsty!

The Lord said He will answer them and not forsake them; He will provide spiritual nourishment for them. He promises to make fruitful what is currently unfruitful, and to put life and vitality where there is currently only barrenness, waste, and death. Afterward, people would see and know that it was the Lord Jesus Christ who had created it all.

You Invited Me In...

Having spent most of my life in the military, I understand the spiritual condition of young military men and women. In Isaiah 43, and verse 8, the Lord instructed us to:

*Lead out those who have eyes but are blind,
 who have ears but are deaf.*

While all these young people have physical eyes and ears, most are spiritually blind and deaf. In verses 10 and 12 God said twice that Yvonne and I were His witnesses. We are His servants, chosen by Him, and sent to let these young people know that He is God. He longs to forgive and cleanse them from their sins, to draw them to Himself, and to make them His own. In Isaiah 43:25, He said,

*I, even I, am He who blots out your transgressions,
 for my own sake, and remembers your sins no more.*

He will provide spiritual nourishment for those He formed for Himself, so they could declare His praise. I was encouraged by the Lord's words in Isaiah 49:8-9, when He said,

*In the time of my favor I will answer you,
    and in the day of salvation I will help you;
I will keep you and will make you
    to be a covenant for the people,
to restore the land
    and to reassign its desolate inheritances,
to say to the captives, 'Come out,'
    and to those in darkness, 'Be free!'*

The work God has prepared for us will result in the salvation of souls! He specifically said that He would help us "in the day

Our Vision

of salvation." As I read those verses, 2 Corinthians 6:1-2 came to my mind, where Paul says:

> *As God's fellow workers we urge you not to receive God's grace in vain. For he says, 'In the time of my favor I heard you, and in the day of salvation I helped you.' I tell you, now is the time of God's favor, <u>now</u> is the day of salvation.*

I believe the day in which we live *is* the day of salvation! As such, the Lord promised to help us in this work. His calling on our lives is to say to young military men and women taken captive by the enemy of their souls, "Come out!"— and to say to those sitting in darkness, "Be free!"

Captives Set Free

Let me explain what I mean by young men and women being taken captive by the enemy of their souls. In 2 Timothy 2:25-26, the Apostle Paul said a minister of the Gospel must gently instruct those who oppose him,

> *...in the hope that God will grant them repentance leading them to a knowledge of the truth, and that they will come to their senses and escape from the trap of the devil, who has **taken them captive** to do his will.*

In Acts 8:23, Luke records Peter's rebuke of Simon the sorcerer, who offered money to buy the ability to lay hands on people to receive the Holy Spirit. Peter said,

> *For I see that you are full of bitterness and **captive to sin***

And in Colossians 2:8, Paul warns his readers,

You Invited Me In...

> *See to it that no one **takes you captive** through hollow and deceptive philosophy, which depends on human tradition and the basic principles of this world rather than on Christ.*

According to these passages, there are three things that can take a person captive. The first is the devil, who lays traps for people, and takes them captive to do his will (and yes, we believe the devil is real and that he actually does that). The second is sin itself (i.e., bitterness, alcoholism, drug addiction, sexual immorality, and a host of other self-defeating attitudes and behaviors). The third is deceptive human philosophies that are based on human traditions and worldly principles.

People will, according to Isaiah 49, verses 8 and 9, be set free. They can, according to 2 Timothy 2:25-26, be instructed in the truth, come to their senses, and be rescued from their captivity.

In the military, many young adults, including those raised in Christian homes, are taken captive by the enemy of their souls. The incredible pressure young military men and women are under often leaves them with little time, energy, or desire to focus on their spiritual lives. The world, the flesh, and the devil all conspire to draw them away from faith in God and away from a personal relationship with Jesus Christ.

However, when I read the words in Isaiah 49, I thought about Jesus' conversation with Peter in Matthew 16:13-20. Where Jesus asked His disciples who people were saying He was. The disciples provided a variety of answers. Then Jesus asked them who *they* believed He was. Peter immediately confessed that Jesus was:

"*...the Christ, the Son of the living God.*"

Our Vision

To which Jesus responded that it was not human intellect or reasoning, but God the Father who revealed that to him. Jesus went on to say,

...on this rock I will build my church, and the gates of hell will not overcome it.

The "rock" Jesus referred to was faith in, and the confession of, Him as the Son of the living God. The gates of hell Jesus referred to are the "bars" and "gates" behind which the devil keeps people imprisoned. In this passage Jesus promised that those gates would not be able to withstand the Church that He would establish. All of this is why Isaiah 49:24-25 is such a powerful word related to our ministry. In it, the Lord asks—and answers—the question:

Can plunder be taken from warriors,
 or captives be rescued from the fierce?
But this is what the Lord says:
 "Yes, captives will be taken from warriors,
  and plunder retrieved from the fierce;
I will contend with those who contend with you,
 and your children I will save.

The heartbeat of our ministry is reaching young servicemen and women with the message of salvation, helping them to initiate and develop a personal relationship with Jesus Christ. The enemy of their souls will not win! God will contend with the enemy, and will rescue these young men and women from the enemy's grasp. The latter part of Isaiah 49:26 summarizes the results of this work:

Then all mankind will know that I the Lord, am your
 Savior, your Redeemer, the Mighty One of Jacob.

You Invited Me In...

In Isaiah 45:1-3, the Lord said,

> *This is what the Lord says to his anointed...*
>   *whose right hand I take hold of...*
> *to open doors before him*
>   *so that gates will not be shut:*
> *I will go before you*
>   *and will level the mountains;*
> *I will **break down gates of bronze***
>   *and **cut through bars of iron**.*
> *I will give you hidden treasures,*
>   *riches stored in secret places,*
> *so that you may know that I am the Lord...*
>   *who summons you by name.*

God promises to break down the "gates of bronze" and cut through the "bars of iron" behind which these young men and women are being held. He also promises to give us "hidden treasures," and "riches stored in secret places." Yvonne and I believe that the young men and women who have been taken captive by the enemy *are* the hidden treasures and riches stored in secret places. In Isaiah 51:14, the Lord promised us that,

> *The cowering prisoners will soon be set free;*
> *they will not die in their dungeon,*
>   *nor will they lack bread.*

Those who have been taken captive by the enemy of their souls will be set free. They will not die in their captivity. Nor will they lack spiritual nourishment. God is not willing that any of these young people should perish, but that *all* of them should come to repentance. In Isaiah 49:9-12, describing those we would reach, the Lord said:

*They will feed beside the roads
  and find pasture on every barren hill.
They will neither hunger nor thirst,
  nor will the desert heat or the sun beat down on them.
He who has compassion on them will guide them
  and lead them beside springs of water.
I will turn all my mountains into roads,
  and my highways will be raised up.
See, they will come from afar—
  some from the north, some from the west...*

The young men and women God brings to us will find spiritual "pasture" and be nourished. They will no longer be spiritually hungry or thirsty, nor will the natural elements destroy them. The Lord said one who has compassion on them will guide them and lead them to springs of water.

Yvonne has had compassion for the military since she was a teenager. I came to know Christ as a result of her compassion. My heart, too, has been filled with the same compassion ever since I accepted Christ as my Savior.

The Lord said He would turn mountains into roads, and raise up highways. He promised to remove obstacles from our path and provide level roads for us. Finally, He said those we reach for Him would come from the north and from the west.

Sons and Daughters

In Isaiah 52:11-14, the Lord said,

*Depart, depart, go out from there!
  Touch no unclean thing!
Come out from it and be pure,
  you who carry the articles of the Lord's house.
But you will not leave in haste
  or go in flight;*

for the Lord will go before you,
　the God of Israel will be your rear guard.
See, my servant will act wisely;
　he will be raised and lifted up and highly exalted.

When we left Grand Junction in June of 2000, to move to Virginia Beach, we didn't make the transition quickly. Yvonne and I discussed and prayed about the decision for a year. At her suggestion, we flew to Virginia Beach to actually put "boots on the ground" to see if God would confirm our sense that He was leading us here.

After spending two weeks in the area, we decided this was where the Lord wanted us. In this passage He said He would go before us (to Virginia), *and* stay behind us as our "rear guard" to take care of the teens we had ministered to in Colorado.

The next passage is the heart of our vision and our ministry. In it, the Lord laid out the future focus of our work. In Isaiah 43:5-6, He said,

Do not be afraid, for I am with you;
　I will bring your children from the east
　and gather you from the west.
I will say to the north, 'Give them up!'
　and to the south, 'Do not hold them back.'
Bring my sons from afar
　and my daughters from the ends of the earth—

And in Isaiah 49:18, He said,

Lift up your eyes and look around;
　all your children gather and come to you.
"As surely as I live," declares the Lord,
　"you will wear them all as ornaments;
　you will put them on, like a bride.

Our Vision

God told us He would bring us children, both *sons* and *daughters*. He was telling us our ministry would be family-oriented—relational. And it has been.

Yvonne and I consider every young military man and woman who comes into our home more than once an adopted "son" or "daughter." These young adults very quickly become part of our extended family. We enjoy building relationships with them, being involved in their lives, and having a positive spiritual influence on them.

God promised to bring them from the "north, south, east, and west" and even from the "ends of the earth." Our ministry has had both a national and international dimension. We take great pride in all of the young people who come through our home. I will share some of the actual statistics concerning who and where these young people came from in a later chapter.

Discipleship

Leading young men and women to faith in Christ is only the beginning of our work. After they make the decision to follow Christ, we try to help them get rooted and grounded in the Word of God. In Isaiah 41:15-16, the Lord spoke through the metaphor of a threshing sledge, saying,

See, I will make you into a threshing sledge,
new and sharp, with many teeth.
You will thresh the mountains and crush them,
and reduce the hills to chaff.
You will winnow them, the wind will pick them up,
and a gale will blow them away.
But you will rejoice in the Lord
and glory in the Holy One of Israel.

The metaphor was a picture of a new, sharp, threshing machine used in Bible days to thresh harvested grain. Threshing machines were used to cut up the straw stalks and separate the edible grain from the inedible chaff. Once the grain and chaff were chopped and separated they were winnowed. Winnowing was the process where the chopped chaff was blown away by the wind.

The metaphor spoke to me about the discipleship process in which I felt God was saying He would use us as His instruments to help young military men and women that had been "harvested," or who had accepted Jesus Christ as their Savior, to grow into mature disciples. God would use us to help them separate old, worldly attitudes and behaviors from their lives, and develop the fruit of the Spirit. These new disciples would cause us to rejoice in the Lord and glorify Jesus, the Holy One of Israel.

Spirit Baptism

Following their salvation, part of the discipleship process is helping our sons and daughters receive the baptism with the Holy Spirit, to empower them as witnesses for Jesus Christ. In Isaiah 44:3-5, God said,

> *For I will pour water on the thirsty land,*
>   *and streams on the dry ground;*
> *I will pour out my Spirit on your offspring,*
>   *and my blessing on your descendants.*
> *They will spring up like grass in a meadow,*
>   *like poplar trees by flowing streams.*
> *Some will say, 'I belong to the Lord';*
>   *others will call themselves by the name of Jacob;*
> *still others will write on their hand, 'The Lord's,'*
>   *and will take the name Israel.*

In these verses, the Lord said four things: The first is that our sons and daughters, hungering and thirsting after righteousness,

Our Vision

would be satisfied by accepting Jesus Christ as their Savior. Second, the Lord would pour out His Spirit on them—baptizing them with the Holy Spirit. Third, they would be as numerous as blades of grass in a meadow. And Fourth, they would call themselves by different names, which we believe means they would belong to different denominations.

As part of our preparation, the Lord said He had put His words in our mouths. In Isaiah 59:21, He said,

"My Spirit, who is on you, will not depart from you, and my words that I have put in your mouth will always be on your lips, on the lips of your children and on the lips of their descendants—from this time on and forever," says the Lord.

Here again God said His Spirit would be upon us, and would not depart from us. He also said His Word that He put in our mouths, would stay with us. And, as we teach it to our sons and daughters, it will remain with them and with their descendants as well.

More Space—Expansion

In Isaiah 49:19-20, the Lord said,

...you will be too small for your people...[your]
  children...will yet say in your hearing,
'This place is too small for us;
  give us more space to live in.'

We've received emails from young servicemen and women who have been through our home, saying they miss us and wish they could find someone who was doing what we do in their new location. Right now, we know of none. When one of our soldiers, sailors, or marines, gets transferred to a base in another

You Invited Me In...

part of the country, we know of no Pentecostal families involved in hospitality house ministry with whom we can connect them. But we believe that will change. In Isaiah 51:1-2 God said,

> *Listen to me, you who pursue righteousness*
> *and who seek the Lord:*
> *Look to the rock from which you were cut*
> *and to the quarry from which you were hewn;*
> *look to Abraham, your father,*
> *and to Sarah, who gave you birth.*
> *When I called him he was only one man,*
> *and I blessed him and made him many.*

Through these verses, God told us that while we were only one couple doing this work right now, He would bless us, multiply us, and make us many. As we cast this vision, God will speak to people around the country and call those He wants involved in this type of military ministry. As those people respond to God's call, the specifics of this vision will apply to them as well as to us. The vision will then move from being a personal one to a broader, shared vision of the future.

Summoning Churches

Survey after survey concludes that people today are biblically illiterate; even people who consider themselves evangelical and born-again Christians. The spiritual darkness is so heavy it is almost palpable. In Isaiah 60:1-2, the Lord said,

> *Arise, shine, for your light has come,*
> *and the glory of the Lord rises upon you.*
> *See, darkness covers the earth*
> *and thick darkness is over the peoples,*
> *but the Lord rises upon you*
> *and his glory appears over you.*

Our Vision

But in contrast to this darkness, the Lord says our light has come and *He* rises upon us. As a result of this light, He said in verse 3 of Isaiah 60:

Nations will come to your light,
  and kings to the brightness of your dawn.

As I thought about the application of this passage to our ministry, the Lord said the word "nations" in our context means "churches." I believe God is saying: Because of the light of the Lord, and His glory that is rising upon us, churches will be drawn to us and to this ministry.
In Isaiah 55:4-5, God said:

See, I have made him a witness to the peoples,
  a ruler and commander of the peoples.
Surely you will summon nations you know not,
  and nations you do not know will come running to you,
because of the Lord your God,
  the Holy One of Israel,
for he has endowed you with splendor.

I understood God to be saying that, as spiritual leaders in the Church, we would contact churches that we did not know and share our vision of Pentecostal hospitality house military ministry. And even though they do not know us, they would respond positively and get involved. All of this would happen because of Jesus Christ (the Holy One of Israel) and the anointing He has placed upon us.

Many Pentecostal churches and pastors do not see the need, nor have the desire or inclination to minister to young military men and women. But God said He would move on their hearts and call them into military ministry. In Isaiah 41:2-4, the Lord said,

You Invited Me In...

*He hands nations over to him
   and subdues kings before him...
He pursues them and moves on unscathed,
   by a path his feet have not traveled before.
Who has done this and carried it through,
   calling forth the generations from the beginning?
I, the Lord—with the first of them
   and with the last—I am he.*

In Isaiah 49:7, the Lord said,

*This is what the Lord says—
   the Redeemer and Holy One of Israel...
Kings will see you and stand up,
   princes will see and bow down,
because of the Lord, who is faithful,
   the Holy One of Israel, who has chosen you.*

God wanted to make sure we knew who was speaking to us. It was Jesus Christ our Redeemer. Here again, in our context, the words "kings" and "rulers" mean "pastors"—and "princes" refer to their "associates." In this passage, God was assuring us that pastors and their associates would see the vision, and they would recognize and acknowledge the need for this ministry.

In Isaiah 49:22-23, the Lord went on to say that there will be those who cooperate with us.

*This is what the Sovereign Lord says:
"See, I will beckon to the nations,
   I will lift up my banner to the peoples;
they will bring your sons in their arms
   and carry your daughters on their hips.
Kings will be your foster fathers,
   and their queens your nursing mothers.*

Our Vision

> *They will bow down before you with their faces to the ground...*
> *Then you will know that I am the Lord;*
> *those who hope in me will not be disappointed."*

In this passage there is an interesting reference to "foster fathers and mothers." As before, I believe the word "kings" means "pastors." Here, I interpret the word "queens" to mean either "their wives" or "other women in their churches." God was telling us that He would lift up His banner to the people, and they would bring our sons and daughters.

But since Yvonne and I cannot be everywhere at the same time, they would not literally bring them to us, but that *they* would carry them. God has promised to raise up "foster parents" in other locations where *our* sons and daughters get stationed, who would care for them. We will see that it is the Lord who is doing this. And because our hope is in Him, we would not be disappointed.

Opposition

Sadly, one of the things God also let me know was that there would be opposition to this work. There would be those who would oppose reaching servicemen and women for Jesus Christ from a Pentecostal perspective. But He has given us a message to proclaim, and He said we are to do it boldly and without fear, just as He told the prophet in Jeremiah 1:17,

> *Get yourself ready! Stand up and say to them whatever I command you. Do not be terrified by them, or I will terrify you before them.*

And in Jeremiah 1:18-19, where He said,

You Invited Me In...

> *Today I have made you a fortified city, an iron pillar and a bronze wall to stand against the whole land—against the kings...its officials, its priests and the people of the land.*

We are to stand strong even in the face of opposition. God was warning us that there would be opposition, but that He would be with us and rescue us:

> *They will fight against you but will not overcome you, for I am with you and will rescue you, declares the Lord.*

In Isaiah 46:3-4 God repeated His promise to sustain and rescue us even into our old age:

> *Listen to me...you whom I have upheld since your birth,*
>   *and have carried since you were born.*
> *Even to your old age and gray hairs*
>   *I am he, I am he who will sustain you.*
> *I have made you and I will carry you;*
>   *I will sustain you and I will rescue you.*

And because of God's promises, we can say with the prophet in Isaiah 50, verse 7,

> *Because the Sovereign Lord helps me,*
>   *I will not be disgraced.*
> *Therefore have I set my face like flint,*
>   *and I know I will not be put to shame.*

He both warned and reassured me, in Isaiah 41:11-14, that,

> *All who rage against you*
>   *will surely be ashamed and disgraced;*

Our Vision

> *those who oppose you*
> *will be as nothing and perish.*
> *Though you search for your enemies,*
> *you will not find them.*
> *Those who wage war against you*
> *will be as nothing at all.*
> *For I am the Lord your God*
> *who takes hold of your right hand*
> *and says to you, "Do not fear; I will help you.*
> *Do not be afraid...for I myself will help you,"*
> *declares the Lord, your Redeemer, the Holy One of Israel.*

In Isaiah 54:14-15, God said that any opposition that arose would not be coming from Him:

> *In righteousness you will be established:*
> *Tyranny will be far from you;*
> *you will have nothing to fear.*
> *Terror will be far removed;*
> *it will not come near you.*
> *If anyone does attack you it will not be my doing;*
> *whoever attacks you will surrender to you.*

And in the latter part of Isaiah 51:7-8, He said,

> *Do not fear the reproach of mere mortals*
> *or be terrified by their insults.*
> *For the moth will eat them up like a garment;*
> *the worm will devour them like wool.*

Finally, in Isaiah 54:16-17, the Lord assured me that He would be with us in this work and would not allow any weapons formed against us to prosper:

> *See, it is I who created the blacksmith*
>   *who fans the coals into flame*
>   *and forges a weapon fit for its work.*
> *And it is I who have created the destroyer to wreak havoc;*
> *no weapon forged against you will prevail,*
>   *and you will refute every tongue that accuses you...*

When God spoke these words to my heart, I immediately thought of 2 Timothy Chapter 2, and verses 15, 20 and 21, where He said I was to do my best to present myself as one approved, a workman who does not need to be ashamed and who correctly handles the Word of Truth. I was to have nothing to do with foolish and stupid arguments, because I know they produce quarrels. And God says I was not to quarrel.

Instead, I was to be kind to everyone and not resentful. I was to gently instruct those who opposed me in the hope that the Lord would grant them repentance leading them to the knowledge of the truth, and that they would come to their senses, escaping from the trap of the devil who had taken them captive to do his will.

Provisions for Ministry

While sitting at my desk in Grand Junction almost two decades ago, God spoke to me through 2 Corinthians 9:6-15, saying:

> *Remember this: Whoever sows sparingly will also reap sparingly, and whoever sows generously will also reap generously....And God is able to bless you abundantly, so that in all things at all times, having all that you need, you will abound in every good work...Now he who supplies seed to the sower and bread for food will also supply and increase your store of seed and will enlarge*

the harvest of your righteousness. You will be enriched in every way so that you can be generous on every occasion, and through us your generosity will result in thanksgiving to God. This service that you perform is not only supplying the needs of the Lord's people but is also overflowing in many expressions of thanks to God. Because of the service by which you have proved yourselves, others will praise God for the obedience that accompanies your confession of the gospel of Christ, and for your generosity in sharing with them and with everyone else. And in their prayers for you their hearts will go out to you, because of the surpassing grace God has given you.

I was blessed by God's affirmation that He was able to make all grace abound to us and that in everything we would have all that we needed to do this work. As the one who supplies seed to the sower and bread for food, He has supplied and increased our store of seed that we sow into others' lives. He has enlarged the harvest of our righteousness: those we have reached for Christ. All of this has been His doing.

Many of the parents of military men and women who have come through our home have told us they thank God for our work. And in their prayers for us, they have told us that their hearts do go out to us because of what we have done for their children.

I believed and received all of that. But in the midst of that passage the Lord said something I had a much harder time believing. He said He would make us rich *in every way*, so that we could be generous on every occasion.

My first thought was "Yea, right! Wow, *that's* wishful thinking!" I had never thought about being rich (monetarily). After all, I know what the Bible says about the love of money

You Invited Me In…

being the root of all evil.[16] But the words in 2 Corinthians 9 really stood out to me. I kept wondering if they were *really* for me, or if I was just imagining things. I finally just dismissed that part of the passage.

That was on a Wednesday.

The following Sunday morning, Yvonne and I were sitting in New Horizon Foursquare Church in Grand Junction, Colorado, when the pastor introduced a guest speaker, Rev. Mike Boland. When the pastor said Rev. Boland was a prophet, I thought, "Oh no, and we're sitting near the front of the church!"

I really hoped he wouldn't call us out. But sure enough, we were the first couple he called forward. We went to the front, and as we did, I thought, "OK, we'll politely cooperate, listen, and then quickly sit down again." I was prepared to dismiss whatever he said. Both Yvonne and I have always been very skeptical of personal prophecies. It's not that we don't believe in them, we are just extremely cautious.

We went forward, and Rev. Boland began praying for us. (What follows is a transcript from the audiotape of the service.)

> "Lord, I thank you for rich grace. And Lord, these people have needed rich grace. But there is no such thing, God, as poor grace. For what you give us is rich grace. When we think of rich grace we think of opulence. We think of more than enough."

Rev. Boland now had my *undivided* attention! He didn't know us, and we didn't know him. So there was no way he could have known what the Lord had spoken to my heart while I was sitting in my office the Wednesday before.

He went on:

---

[16] 1 Timothy 6:10

Our Vision

"But then Lord, did not the scripture say to us that part of your purpose in coming to the earth was to make us more than conquerors? And, Lord, there have been times in their lives when they would have been satisfied with the victory. But it has always been your purpose to give them more than that. And, Lord, I thank you for the depth that they have been able to attain; because they have gone to depths. They have known certain struggles and certain difficulties. And in those struggles they have understood that your presence was truly their salvation.

"Now, Lord, I want you to begin to rearrange in them certain things that they think about and that they perceive about themselves, Lord, as a deep work. Not as a shallow work, but as a deep work, Lord. Lord, I want you to work in my brother's mind and bring him to that place of absolute peace; that place, Lord, where he's not warring with his past, and not warring with some of the obligations that he's made in the past, that have been obligations after the flesh, that in the spirit he became troubled with. But, Lord, remind him that you have, even in recent times, worked in him to renew him.

"And, Lord, that though it is extremely important that we be true to our word, Lord, there are words that must be repented of and turned from. Even if we have to go back and we have to make our apologies; obligations that have to be broken because they were made after a worldly fashion. And, Lord, that your purpose in us is to cause us to be whole, but also to find our place on this earth in you.

"Lord, I ask you to make my brother, in the natural, a very successful man. Show favor upon the things that he is attached to. Show great favor. And, Lord, begin to cause the kinds of effects that he's looking for to come to pass. Lord, begin to cause, Lord, even what he puts his hand to, Lord, to take on, Lord, just a very established condition. And, Lord, that which is temporary and that which doesn't seem well established, Lord, I just declare in the name of Jesus, that it will become well established. And he will not look at the things he is involved in, participating in, as if they were temporary, but he will begin to see the permanence of the work that God is doing, by the Spirit.

"And, Lord, I thank you that, Lord, that this precious sister who stands before you right now, Lord, is someone who's sought your face to know what it means to be able to surrender everything to you and know what Lordship is. And, Lord, she's looked over her walk and she has seen times and places and ways, Lord, in which, Lord, she's given things over to you but had a tendency to come and take them back, and carry burdens, Lord, that she had rolled over onto you, allowing the enemy to deceive her into thinking that she must continue to carry those specific burdens. For, Lord, I declare, in the name of Jesus, that burdens rolled over on the Lord are to be left with Him. And I just separate from her all those burdens that she picks back up, and carries, at various seasons and various times, through worry.

"And I cast down worry in Jesus' name, and I say that that tendency to pick things up and let them just rest in the mind bringing a certain weariness to the mind, I just speak to that weariness of mind and I say, 'be loosed and released from that burden, knowing that these things are rolled over on the Lord, and that He is working concerning the things that we have presented to Him.'

"And, Lord, I say to both of them: and I want you all to really hear this, this is important. In my spirit, I know that you've given up on some things; some goals, some dreams, some visions. The Lord says 'That which you have given up on, I have not released, and I have not let go.' For those things which you have given up on, to some degree are those things that the Lord God Himself put into your spirit. And the Lord says, 'I will yet come with blessings in my hand. I will yet come with the power of restoration, to bring things to life that seem

Our Vision

dead. I will resuscitate your dreams and I will rescue your vision, and cause it to flow with newness.'

"And know this, the Lord says, 'I call for a spring season, a season of life, a season of things coming into being. Not a season of things where you've felt like in many ways that many of your dreams, many of your purposes, and even uses as believers were literally on the back shelf, on the back burner.' The Lord says, 'I'm bringing it all up to the front of the stove. And when the pot begins to boil just remember that it's being cooked through and through. And that, a precious harvest of blessing. I will give you that which you will be able to give away. I will not merely come with provision, I will come with ample provision,' saith the Lord. 'For if you only get that which is bare necessity provision then it will not be enough to fulfill the purposes that I, the Lord your God, have for you. Have I not set you in the kingdom to be as those who give, as those who give generously? And I will so cause it to be that you will rejoice in the blessings of your God.'

"Lord, in the name of Jesus I just loose blessing right now. I just pray in the name of Jesus that power from on high would just rest, Lord, upon these right now in the name of Jesus. And that fresh anointing, Lord, would just begin to come, and, Lord, let them know what it means, Lord, when you said 'a spring season.' Lord, let the joy of the Lord rise up in them, and let gladness begin to work in them, Lord, as a new and precious work is done. And Lord, I say that all their hurts and all their wounds are cast down, and that worry is cast down in the name of Jesus. And rejoicing for the favor of God is upon you. We declare this is so in Jesus' name. Amen."

Humanly speaking, God knew the promise He made to me in 2 Corinthians 9:6-15 was so huge it would be difficult if not impossible for me to believe. So He sent a prophet I had never met, to confirm the words He had spoken to my heart. Rev.

You Invited Me In...

Boland's prophecy was an incredibly powerful confirmation of what the Lord said to me the previous Wednesday! After that experience I *knew* God had spoken those words to *me*.

That was 24 years ago.

Are we rich?

In many ways, we are.

But are we rich financially?

No, not yet.

But, by faith, I believe God is going to fulfill that promise too! How and when, I have no idea. But I have been learning to walk by faith and not by sight. God said He would do all of this, so I would know it was Him who summoned me by name. In the meantime, God has been helping us practice being generous with what we already have.

But God didn't just speak about provision for ministry through 2 Corinthians, He also spoke to me about it through Isaiah 60:4-5, in which the Lord mentioned our "sons" and "daughters" in connection with His provision saying,

> *Lift up your eyes and look about you:*
>   *All assemble and come to you;*
> *your sons come from afar,*
>   *and your daughters are carried on the hip.*
> *Then you will look and be radiant,*
>   *your heart will throb and swell with joy;*
> *the wealth on the seas will be brought to you,*
>   *to you the riches of the nations will come.*

I've said it before: Yvonne and I grow to love the servicemen and women who come into our home and into our lives. Reaching them for Jesus Christ does make our hearts "throb" and "swell with joy." It is God who brings us together with them, who carries them to us from afar.

Our Vision

In this passage, God tells us that churches (nations) will help provide the necessary finances to accomplish this work. And in verse 7 He says these finances:

> *...will be accepted as offerings on my altar, and I will adorn my glorious temple.*

In verse 9, the Lord even says our sons and daughters would be part of the provision He has in store, saying,

> *in the lead are the ships...*
> *bringing your children from afar,*
> *with their silver and gold,*
> *to the honor of the Lord your God,*
> *the Holy One of Israel,*
> *for he has endowed you with splendor.*

Remember, this vision was originally given to me in 1993, while I was living in Grand Junction, Colorado—long before we moved to Virginia Beach to minister to the military. But now, 25 years later, I realize how prophetic the words of the vision were—and still are.

The focus of our ministry in the Norfolk-Virginia Beach area is primarily on the sailors in the Navy, so the sailors we reach on the ships homeported here can be thought of as "in the lead." I believe that as this ministry expands, soldiers, marines and airmen all across this country will be won to Christ. In this verse, God says these young men and women will come with their silver and gold, in honor of the Lord Jesus Christ. Once again, all of this will happen, the Lord says, because of the splendor with which He has endowed us.

In Isaiah 60:10-14, God said,

You Invited Me In...

> *...in favor I will show you compassion.*
> *Your gates will always stand open,*
> *they will never be shut, day or night,*
> *so that people may bring you the wealth of the nations...*
> *to adorn my sanctuary;*
> *and I will glorify the place for my feet.*

I believe this passage, as applied to our ministry, is again talking about the financial support of churches (nations) that catch the vision and get involved with Pentecostal hospitality house military ministry. That support, the Lord says, will be viewed by Him as adorning the place of His sanctuary and bringing glory to Him.

I said this earlier, but I think it bears repeating here to allay any misunderstanding. Several years ago, the Lord told me He was able to make all grace abound to me, so that in all things, and at all times, having all that we need, we would abound in every good work.

The One who scatters abroad His gifts to the poor, whose righteousness endures forever, and who supplies seed to the sower and bread for food, said He would also supply and increase our store of seed and enlarge the harvest of our righteousness. He said we would be made rich in every way so that we could be generous on every occasion, and that our generosity would result in thanksgiving to Him.

All this talk about wealth is not merely for the sake of becoming wealthy, but for the ability to be generous. God said the service we are performing is not only supplying the needs of His people, but also overflowing in many expressions of thanks to Him. And because of the service by which we have proved ourselves, the Lord said men would praise *Him* for the obedience that accompanies our confession of the gospel, and for our generosity in sharing with them and with everyone else.

Our Vision

God said their hearts would go out to us in their prayers for us because of the grace *He* has given us. God knew it would be hard for me to accept all of this, so He sent a prophet to *confirm* what He said. God's promises are not "yea" and "nay," but "Yea" and "Amen" in Christ Jesus. At this point, I am still trusting Him, and believing that He will fulfill even this promise.

I found Isaiah 60 and verse 17 really interesting. In it, the Lord said He would reverse our fortunes. He said,

> *Instead of bronze I will bring you gold,*
> *and silver in place of iron.*
> *Instead of wood I will bring you bronze,*
> *and iron in place of stones.*

Finally, in verse 21 the Lord said,

> *Then all your people will be righteous*
> *and they will possess the land forever.*
> *They are the shoot I have planted,*
> *the work of my hands,*
> *for the display of my splendor*

In these words, He declared that righteousness would characterize the servicemen and women we reach for Christ. They will take possession of their spiritual land. They will be the shoot that God has planted, the result of the work of *His* hands. All of this will be for His splendor. And in verse 22, He said those we reach for Christ will go on to reach others for Him as well:

> *The least of you will become a thousand,*
> *the smallest a mighty nation.*
> *I am the Lord;*
> *in its time I will do this swiftly.*

4

WHY HOSPITALITY?

In the 18 years that Yvonne and I have been ministering to the military in our home, one of the most enjoyable moments is when a young serviceman or woman comes through our front door, smiles and says, "Wow! It's been so long since I've been in a real home!"

In Matthew 25:35, Jesus said,

I was hungry and you gave me something to eat, I was thirsty and you gave me something to drink, I was a stranger and you invited me in.

Jesus was talking about ministering to the needs of others through hospitality. In the American Dictionary of the English Language[17] the word hospitality is defined as, "The act or practice of receiving and entertaining strangers or guests without reward, or with kind and generous liberality."

---

[17] *American Dictionary of the English Language*, s.v. "hospitality," accessed March 13, 2018, http://webstersdictionary1828.com/Dictionary/hospitality.

You Invited Me In...

For Yvonne and me, hospitality becomes real and practical as we open our home and provide 18- to 25-year-old sailors, soldiers, marines, and airmen a safe and comfortable home and family environment where they can relax and get away from the pressures of military life for a few hours each week. Providing this environment helps us develop personal relationships, and opens the door for us to share the gospel of Jesus Christ with them.

Earlier I referred to our ministry as a "hospitality house military ministry." The key here is the word *hospitality*. In Romans 12, Paul talks about a variety of functions and gifts operating in the body of Christ. And in verse 13, he says, "Practice hospitality." In this chapter, I want to show you why, from a biblical perspective, hospitality motivates us and why it is essential in military ministry.

Hospitality in the Old Testament

The concept of hospitality is a significant theme that runs throughout the Bible, in both Old and New Testaments. In the book of Genesis, God called Abraham to leave his family and his country and go to a land that God would show him.[18] Abraham was obedient, left his relatives and his country, and went to the land of Canaan. Ultimately, the nation of Israel came from Abraham and his descendants.

As you read the story of Abraham and the development of the Israelite nation, it is obvious that the Israelites knew what it meant to be aliens and strangers in a foreign land. And because of this communal experience, God forbade the Israelites from mistreating the aliens or strangers who lived among them. God expected the Israelites' collective memory as mistreated and oppressed strangers in a foreign land to influence their treatment of strangers (Exodus 22:21, 23:9).

---

[18] Genesis 12:1-4

Why Hospitality?

Not only were they to refrain from negative behavior toward strangers; they were to be proactive in treating them positively. Strangers were to be treated as native-born Israelites, and were to be loved by them. God wanted the Israelites to know that it was He Who required them to treat strangers correctly. But He knew the requirement would be difficult for them to implement, so He put the full weight of His authority behind it by adding, "I am the Lord your God" (Leviticus 19:34).

The prohibition against mistreating the stranger, and the proactive principle of loving them, was not based solely on God's authority, but on His character and His relationship with the Israelites. The Israelites believed in God. But, according to Deuteronomy 10:12-22, it wasn't enough for them to simply *believe* in Him; they were to *love* Him with all their hearts and souls.

They were to love God because He loved them first. As a result, the Israelites' love for strangers, and their ethical treatment of them, was to be based on their relationship with God. On God's character, His love for them, and on His ethical treatment of the stranger. In other words, the Israelites were to imitate God in their treatment of aliens in the land of Israel.

In Deuteronomy 26:12-13, God required the Israelites to take a portion of the produce of their land (10 percent) and bring it before the priests as a thanksgiving offering. This was called the law of the tithes and first fruits. This tithe was to be distributed among several groups of people, including the Levites, the aliens, and the fatherless and widows. It was not just for the needs of the religious leaders, the priests and Levites, but also for the provision of food for the aliens.

In Genesis 18, Abraham practiced hospitality toward three strangers that appeared to him one hot summer afternoon. He invited them to come into his tent, and prepared a meal for them. The three strangers turned out to be three divine messengers: two angels and the Lord Himself.

Through this direct encounter with God, Abraham received a divine reaffirmation of the promise that Sarah would have a baby, and that it would finally come the following year. Twenty-four years earlier, God had promised they would have a baby; and now He was telling them it was about to happen. This encounter between God and Abraham also resulted in the deliverance of Abraham's nephew Lot from the destruction of Sodom and Gomorrah.

In the Old Testament God's testimony of a man named Job was that he was blameless and upright. In one of his responses to his critical friends, Job based his claim to having lived a proper and acceptable life before God on the fact that he practiced hospitality. He had never allowed strangers to sleep in the streets; his doors had always been open to them (Job 31:32).

By the time of the prophet Isaiah, the Israelites had institutionalized many of their religious practices, and prided themselves on their ritualized fasting. At one point, the prophet records the Israelites' wondering why God was not taking notice of them while they fasted. Through the prophet, God told the Israelites that He *was* taking notice of their fasting. But He was not pleased. He reminded them of His mandate for exercising hospitality and concern for others.

In Isaiah 58:6-7, He chastised them concerning their idea of fasting, and the way they behaved during their fasts. He said,

Yet on the day of your fasting, you do as you please
  and exploit all your workers.
Your fasting ends in quarreling and strife,
  and in striking each other with wicked fists.

The Israelites' behavior during and after their fasts displeased God. And through Isaiah, God told the Israelites what the proper elements of a fast were. He said,

Is not this the kind of fasting I have chosen:
to loose the chains of injustice
* and untie the cords of the yoke,*
to set the oppressed free
* and break every yoke?*
Is it not to share your food with the hungry
* and to provide the poor wanderer with shelter—*
when you see the naked, to clothe them,
* and not to turn away from your own flesh and blood?*

These were the exact opposite of the things the Israelites were doing.

From this brief overview it is easy to see how important practicing hospitality toward the alien was to God in the Old Testament. It was a practice that had to come from the heart, based on a person's relationship with Yahweh. It was not just an external ritual to be followed.

Hospitality in the New Testament

In the New Testament, the word hospitality comes from the Greek word φιλοχενοσ, or philoxenos, and reflects two Greek words: philos (love - for a friend) and xenos (foreign or alien), and literally means: "love of strangers."

Just as the command in the Old Testament to treat the alien properly was based on the character of God the Father—Yahweh–and the Israelites' love relationship with Him, so in the New Testament, the command to treat the stranger properly is also based on the character of God, in this case, God the Son—Jesus—and the Christian's love relationship with Him.

The Jewish Shema

Let me explain the significance of that transition. In Jesus' ministry, the Jewish authorities repeatedly tried to trap Jesus in His words. Their attempts revolved around what the Israelites

You Invited Me In...

call the Shema, or the "greatest commandment" in the Law. The Jews understood the Shema to say,

> *Hear, O Israel: The Lord our God, the Lord is one. Love the Lord your God with all your heart and with all your soul and with all your strength.*[19]

They believed that their God had no son. Yet Jesus repeatedly said He was God's Son. As such, He was claiming, in His essence, to be God, and that the Jews were to love and obey *Him* (John 15).

In Matthew 22:34-39, the Pharisees had gathered together, and an expert in the law came to "test" Jesus, asking Him what the "greatest" commandment in the Law was. It was obvious from the way the question was asked, that the Pharisees were anticipating an answer from Jesus that would contradict the Shema. But He did not contradict it, and actually quoted it correctly from Deuteronomy 6:5, and then added the commonly accepted second greatest commandment in the Law by quoting Leviticus 19:18. Jesus said:

> *Love the Lord your God with all your heart and with all your soul and with all your mind. This is the first and greatest commandment. And the second is like it: 'Love your neighbor as yourself.'*[20]

Then Jesus turned to the Pharisees and questioned them. He asked them whose son the Christ (Messiah) was. When they responded that He was the son of David, Jesus asked them how it was possible for the Messiah to be David's son when David, speaking by the Spirit, called the Messiah "Lord" (Psalm 110:1)? Jesus' challengers were silent and had no answer.

---

[19] Deuteronomy 6:4-5
[20] Matthew 22:34-39

Why Hospitality?

Jesus knew David was referring to Him prophetically. Because the Messiah would be the human descendant of David, David could call Him his son. And, because the Messiah would be fully divine, David could call Him "Lord." Prophetically, David was saying that the coming Messiah would be fully human *and* fully divine.

In this counter-challenge to the Pharisees, Jesus was applying Psalm 110:1 to Himself. He was asserting that He was the long-awaited Jewish Messiah. He was both the fully human son of David, and the fully divine Son of God. Jesus was claiming to be God, and was asserting that He was the fulfillment of the Jewish Scriptures as the Messiah Who would sit on David's throne.

Thus, in this exchange with the Jewish religious leaders, Jesus was saying that the Jewish Shema applied to Himself—as God. They were to love Him, Jesus, with all their heart, soul, mind, and strength. Their love was to be directed vertically toward Him; and then out of that divine love relationship, their love was to flow horizontally toward their fellow man. In Luke's account of this exchange (Luke 10:29-37), Jesus added the parable of the Good Samaritan, illustrating what this love for a "neighbor" was supposed to look like when it was actually put into practice.

In the Old Testament, the Israelites' treatment of the stranger was to be based on the character of God the Father and their love relationship with Him. In the New Testament, the Christian's treatment of the stranger is to be based on the character of God the Son and their love relationship with Him.

Hospitality and the Judgment

In Matthew 24 and 25, Jesus taught about His second coming, the time when He would return to earth and sit on His throne in judgment of the people living on the earth. In Matthew 25:31-43, He said,

You Invited Me In...

> "When the Son of Man comes in his glory, and all the angels with him, he will sit on his throne in heavenly glory. All the nations will be gathered before him, and he will separate the people one from another as a shepherd separates the sheep from the goats....
>
> "Then the King will say to those on his right, 'Come, you who are blessed by my Father; take your inheritance, the kingdom prepared for you since the creation of the world. For I was hungry and you gave me something to eat, I was thirsty and you gave me something to drink, I was a stranger and you invited me in, I needed clothes and you clothed me, I was sick and you looked after me, I was in prison and you came to visit me...I tell you the truth, whatever you did for one of the least of these brothers of mine, you did for me.'
>
> "Then he will say to those on his left, 'Depart from me, you who are cursed, into the eternal fire prepared for the devil and his angels. For I was hungry and you gave me nothing to eat, I was thirsty and you gave me nothing to drink, I was a stranger and you did not invite me in, I needed clothes and you did not clothe me, I was sick and in prison and you did not look after me.'

The criteria or basis for Jesus' judgment will be whether or not we saw the needs of those around us and ministered to them. God came to earth, became a human being, modeled servanthood for us, and suffered and died a horrible death on the cross for our sins. Then He rose from the dead. He did all of this so we might be reconciled to God. In this passage in Matthew, God set the criteria for divine judgment as ministering to the needs of others.

Does that mean salvation can be earned by works of kindness to our neighbor rather than simple faith in Jesus Christ alone?

Why Hospitality?

The answer to that question is: No, not at all! God asks Christians in James 2:14,

What good is it, my brothers and sisters, if someone claims to have faith but has no deeds? Can such faith save them?

The answer follows in verses 15-17, through an illustration:

Suppose a brother or a sister is without clothes and daily food. If one of you says to them, 'Go in peace; keep warm and well fed,' but does nothing about their physical needs, what good is it? In the same way, faith by itself, if it is not accompanied by action, is dead.

So Jesus' judgment of the people who did not minister to the needs of those around them was, in actuality, a judgment of their *lack of faith*. Jesus' judgment was pronounced on them because their faith was demonstrated to be dead. When we practice hospitality and minister to the needs of those around us, we are actually ministering to Christ Himself.

Ministry in Houses

In the Gospels, Jesus' ministry was often conducted in people's homes. For example, in Matthew 9:10, Jesus went to Matthew the tax collector's home and ate dinner with him. In Mark 5:38, Jesus went to the home of Jairus the synagogue ruler and raised his daughter from the dead. In Luke 5:18, while Jesus was in a house teaching, four men lowered a paralyzed man on a mat through the roof of the house, so Jesus could heal him. And in Luke 19:5-9, Jesus went to Zacchaeus' home and ate with him, the outcome of which was Zacchaeus' salvation.

Many of the major events recorded in the New Testament took place in houses, and very possibly, private homes. For

You Invited Me In...

example: The Last Supper, as recorded in Luke 22:10-12, took place in the upper room of a house. Jesus' appearance to the disciples on Easter evening, recorded in John 20:19, was in a room whose doors were locked, again, very possibly, a private home. And on the Day of Pentecost, in Acts 2:2, 120 followers of Jesus were gathered together in one place—in the upper room of a house.

The conversion of a woman named Lydia in Acts 16:11-15 is an excellent case in point. This woman believed the gospel message Paul shared with her, received salvation through faith in Jesus Christ, and as a result of her changed heart, immediately offered to minister to Paul and his companions. She invited them to stay in her home. She and her whole family were saved and baptized in water.

In the early church, when believers were still part of the Jewish temple community, the scripture says they met in the temple and in individual homes:

They devoted themselves to the apostles' teaching and to the fellowship, to the breaking of bread and to prayer.... Every day they continued to meet together in the temple courts. They broke bread in their homes and ate together with glad and sincere hearts, praising God and enjoying the favor of all the people. And the Lord added to their number daily those who were being saved.[21]

This description is repeated in Acts 5:42:

Day after day, in the temple courts and from house to house, they never stopped teaching and proclaiming the good news that Jesus is the Christ.

---

[21] Acts 2:42-47

Why Hospitality?

In Acts, Luke tells the story of Priscilla and Aquila, who heard Apollos, a man who knew the scriptures, speak in the temple. However, he only had a limited understanding about the Lord, so Priscilla and Aquila:

...invited him to their home and explained to him the way of God more adequately.[22]

Luke goes on to record Paul's farewell to the Ephesian elders in which the apostle said,

You know that I have not hesitated to preach anything that would be helpful to you, but have taught you publicly and from house to house.[23]

When the gospel message was first presented to the Gentiles, it was presented in the home of Cornelius the centurion. Cornelius was a Roman military officer who had been commanded by an angel to send for the Apostle Peter. Luke records the story in Acts, Chapter 10. In verses 24 and 33, Luke says,

The following day he [Peter] arrived in Caesarea. Cornelius was expecting them and had called together his relatives and close friends... 'So I sent for you immediately, and it was good of you to come. Now we are all here in the presence of God to listen to everything the Lord has commanded you to tell us.'[24]

While Peter was preaching the gospel message to those assembled in Cornelius' home, the message was believed and

---

[22] Acts 18:26.
[23] Acts 20:20.
[24] Acts 10:24, 33.

received, and immediately the Holy Spirit filled all who were present.

The night Peter was miraculously delivered from prison, Luke records that Peter:

> *...went to the house of Mary the mother of John, also called Mark, where many people had gathered and were praying.*[25]

In Acts 16, Paul and his traveling companions were miraculously delivered from their prison bondage in Philippi. The terrified jailer was about to commit suicide because of what his superiors would see as dereliction of duty. When he realized his prisoners had not escaped, he asked what he had to do to be saved.

Paul responded that he must "believe on the Lord Jesus Christ."[26] The apostle spoke the Word of the Lord to him and to the others in his house, after which the jailer and his whole family believed and were baptized in water. The jailer set a meal before them and was filled with joy because he and his whole family came to believe.

While in Rome, the Apostle Paul rented his own house for two years, and welcomed all who came to see him. He preached boldly about the kingdom of God, and taught about the Lord Jesus Christ, without being hindered.[27]

In his epistles, Paul exhorted his readers to pursue the love of strangers.[28] And he made the love of strangers (hospitality) a qualification for an overseer or pastor in the Church.[29]

---

[25] Acts 12:12.
[26] Acts 16:31.
[27] Acts 28:30-31.
[28] Romans 12:13.
[29] 1 Timothy 3:12, Titus 1:8.

Why Hospitality?

As intense persecution arose against Christians, many having their homes and belongings confiscated by the state, the practice of hospitality became even more significant. In spite of the suffering that the believers in the book of Hebrews were experiencing, the author exhorted them not to forget to entertain or "love strangers" (φιλοχενιασ).[30]

The passage in Hebrews 13:2-3 is similar to the passage in Matthew 25:35-36, and includes the exhortation to visit those in prison, perhaps because the disciples were suffering in prison as a result of their proclamation of the gospel message. Included here is an additional revelation that some, while practicing hospitality, had unknowingly entertained angels. The writer may have been recalling Abraham and his three visitors in Genesis 18.

Finally, in practicing hospitality, a person's attitude is also important. In his first epistle, the Apostle Peter admonished his readers, some of whom were suffering for the cause of Christ, to be hospitable to one another. But he noted, they were to do it without grumbling.[31]

Because hospitality was mandated by God, it could be done out of a sense of legalistic or moral obligation. Hospitality could be shown with a complaining, negative attitude, rather than out of love for Jesus Christ and for others. So, Peter exhorted his readers to love each other deeply from the heart[32] because it was out of this love that true biblical hospitality was to be extended.

Hospitality and Military Ministry

So, how important is a comfortable home and family environment to the servicemen and women we contact? Periodically, we receive emails from some of them answering that question. One female sailor wrote to us and said:

---

[30] Hebrews 13:2.
[31] 1 Peter 4:9.
[32] 1 Peter 4:8.

"It has been a long year and I was starting to give up! Sometimes I feel like God just let go. I know in my mind and in my heart that this is a lie and the more I surround myself with the truth the more I am encouraged! Honestly your home has been a HUGE breath of fresh air and I love being in your home. Thank you so much for this special blessing and I thank you for your encouragement! God bless you both."

Another time, we received an email from a young man who had been attending a Navy school when he came to our home who said:

"Emotionally I felt that most of the people that were running the school were against me.... I often got pulled out of my...classes to be chewed out by senior instructors for trivial things.... I hate judging [Virginia] and its surrounding environs but it seemed to be an ugly place. Your home and your thoughts were the only solace I was truly finding anywhere.... Many of my classmates and people at school found solace in drinking. Religion hasn't been a strong point for many of us. I felt that God had sent you many times to watch after me and others.... I felt that I had a safe place at your home. Not only on lonely Sundays but when I graduated and thought that I was going to sleep at the airport, and you let me stay. When you visited me in [my next command]...I wasn't feeling the greatest.... If your house is empty just remember that a piece of me is still there."

So providing a safe, comfortable home and family environment for military men and women while they're away from their own families is very important. They appreciate it. Their families appreciate it. And their military commands appreciate it.

Why Hospitality?

Yvonne and I love hearing them say, "I feel like I'm part of a real family again." But not only is it important for *them*, Jesus' words come flooding back to my mind:

Lord, when did we see you a stranger and invite you in? The King will reply, I tell you the truth, whatever you did for one of the least of these brothers of mine, YOU DID FOR ME.[33]

This then is the biblical concept of hospitality, and the motivation for our approach to military ministry. My hope, as you've read the pages of this chapter, is that God may have spoken to you through His Word. If you live in a military community, perhaps the Holy Spirit has spoken to you about practicing hospitality toward strangers wearing the uniform of our nation. Perhaps you've heard the Holy Spirit whisper, "Invite them in..."

---

[33] Matthew 25:40.

5

MAKING CONTACT

God has been faithful. He has been, and *is*, fulfilling the vision He gave us. Let me share a few of the details of what has happened. Geographically, Yvonne and I minister in the Norfolk-Virginia Beach area of eastern Virginia, an area with approximately 162,000 active duty military personnel on more than 17 military bases. We reach out to men and women stationed on four of those bases: Oceana Naval Air Station; the Oceana/Dam Neck Annex; Joint Expeditionary Base Little Creek/Fort Story; and the Norfolk Naval Station with the ships that are homeported there.

In the 18 years that we've ministered here, we've had 565 people in our home. And yes, we keep track! We have each person who comes into our home fill out a page in our guest book (see the example on the following page). We record their visit in order to remember who they are, maintain contact with them, and pray for them. Yvonne and I arrange each page alphabetically in a loose leaf binder, and use them as a prayer list to pray regularly, by name, for every person who has been in our home.

Please Sign Our Guestbook

Date: _____

Name: _____

Rate/Rank: _____ Branch of Service: _____

Local Address: _____

City: _____ State: _____ Zip: _____

Telephone: _____

Email Address: _____

Home State: _____

Birthday: _____

Anniversary: _____

Religious/Church Background: _____

Food Allergies? _____

Hobbies/Interests: _____

Making Contact

Remember, through Isaiah 43, verses 5 and 6 God said:

Do not be afraid, for I am with you;
  I will bring your children from the east
  and gather you from the west.
I will say to the north, 'Give them up!'
  and to the south, 'Do not hold them back.'
Bring my sons from afar
  and my daughters from the ends of the earth—[34]

And in Micah 7, verses 11 and 12, He said:

The day for building your walls will come, the day for extending your boundaries. In that day people will come to you...from sea to sea and from mountain to mountain.[35]

In fulfillment of God's promise that He would give us "sons" and "daughters," we've had 400 active duty service members in our home: 291 men and 109 women. God said He would bring them from the north, south, east and west, and even from the ends of the earth. At the time of this writing, the servicemen and women who have been in our home have come from 46 states, from Virginia in the east, and Hawaii in the west; Maine in the north, and Florida in the south.

Internationally, they've come from 7 different countries: from Canada in the north, to Brazil in the south; from the Philippines in the west, and Kenya, Africa, in the east. The servicemen from these other nations include 8 sailors from Brazil, a Navy chaplain from Latvia, and a former fighter pilot from Poland. We have indeed been blessed with a "global" ministry, right from our living room!

---

[34] Isaiah 43:5-6.
[35] Micah 7:11-12.

You Invited Me In...

An unexpected blessing over the years has been the opportunity to minister to the extended families of some of these service members. We've had 73 military dependents (civilian spouses and children), 64 extended family members (mothers, fathers, grandparents, brothers and sisters), and 28 civilian friends of service members in our home.

Another blessing that we didn't expect was the calming effect our ministry would have on the parents of the young men and women who have been through our home. We've received many emails over the years from parents of the young men and women we have ministered to, thanking us for reaching out to their sons and daughters. Whether their children came to our home or not, many mothers have told us it gave them comfort just to know there was someone here who was *trying* to reach out to them. It's been a blessing to know that by reaching out to these young men and women, we indirectly help calm the fears and anxieties of their parents.

The young people who come into our home quickly become like family to us. We tell all of them that they are guests only the first time they come into our home. If they come back, we "adopt" them and they become part of our family.

God told us our adopted sons and daughters would call themselves by different names. In Isaiah 44:5 He said,

> *Some will say, 'I belong to the Lord';*
> *others will call themselves by the name of Jacob;*
> *still others will write on their hand, 'The Lord's,'*
> *and will take the name Israel.*[36]

We understood that to mean they would belong to different denominations. And so far, the servicemen and women who have been involved in our ministry have come from 36 different

---

[36] Isaiah 44:5.

denominations. God's Word is being fulfilled just as He told us it would:

> *The word of the Lord came to me: 'What do you see, Jeremiah?' 'I see the branch of an almond tree,' I replied. The Lord said to me, 'You have seen correctly, for I am watching to see that my word is fulfilled.'*[37]

Prayer

Many people ask us *how* we initially make contact with the servicemen and women we invite into our home. I explain that over the past 18 years, we've made contact with them in many different ways. But the *first* thing we do is pray that God will open doors for us and bring us together with those He wants us to minister to. In Revelation 3:7-8 He told us:

> *These are the words of him who is holy and true, who holds the key of David. What he opens no one can shut, and what he shuts no one can open. I know your deeds. See, I have placed before you an open door that no one can shut.*

We've learned that when we get complacent and don't pray as we should, asking God to make these connections, the contacts gradually stop and the men and women quit coming over. When that happens, we know we have to start praying again. God then begins to bring them back again.

I can't stress enough how important this is, and how much we believe that God is the "Prime Mover" in this ministry. He is the One Who makes this ministry happen, and Who makes the connections for us!

---

[37] Jeremiah 1:11-12.

Prayer Walking

One form our prayers take is what Yvonne and I call "prayer walking." We select a base in the area, go there, park the car, and literally walk the streets, praying for the people stationed on that base. We pray for their salvation, for their families and their relationships. We pray for their ability to do their jobs well, for their safety while performing their duties, and whatever else God brings to our minds to pray about. Sometimes we can't walk, so we drive around a base and pray while we drive. We humorously call that "prayer driving."

Networking With Military Ministries

While Yvonne and I were still pastoring in Colorado, we became members of the Christian Military Fellowship and the Officer's Christian Fellowship, two national organizations that minister to the military. Since there were almost no military personnel stationed in Grand Junction, and we wanted to be involved in military ministry in some way, we listed ourselves in their ministry directories as "hospitality contacts." That meant active duty, reserve, and retired military members of those organizations who were traveling through Grand Junction could call and schedule an overnight stay with us. If we traveled to other places in the country, we could do the same.

When we first visited Virginia Beach to investigate the area and decide whether we were going to move here, we contacted two families from those organizations: Noel and Meryl Dawes, and Steve and Pegeen Stougard. The Dawes and the Stougards each hosted us for a week during our initial visit to the Norfolk-Virginia Beach area. Noel was a retired British Army officer; and Steve and Pegeen were active duty Navy pilots.

The Stougards and the Dawes made us feel extremely welcome. The Stougards introduced us to the Norfolk area and the Norfolk Naval Base where they were stationed. The Dawes

Making Contact

even trusted us to stay in their house while they were away for the first three days!

The Dawes were actively involved in many areas of military ministry in the Norfolk-Virginia Beach area, and introduced us to many of the people and Christian military ministry groups with whom they were involved. Including, for example, every Tuesday and Thursday morning, Noel and Meryl met for prayer and fellowship with the Navy chaplains at the Oceana Naval Air Station. They introduced us to the chaplains on our initial visit, and then invited us to join them regularly when we moved here.

Chapel Attendance

After moving to the area we began attending Sunday morning worship services at the Navy chapel at the Oceana Naval Air Station—Dam Neck Annex. There, we introduced ourselves to young sailors who were attending various Navy schools, and invited them to our house for a home-cooked meal after chapel services.

Later, in 2003, we began attending the chapel at Naval Amphibious Base Little Creek, where we invited soldiers, sailors, and marines, most of whom were attending the Navy School of Music, to our home.

Ministry Website

We felt the need for an online presence as well. So I developed a website for our ministry that connected us with servicemen and women and their families around the world. I posted lots of pictures of our activities.

The servicemen and women told their parents about their pictures. And their parents visited the website to see the pictures of their sons and daughters, and often contacted us, telling us how much they appreciated seeing the pictures of their children involved in our activities. Many said our pictures were the only ones they had seen of their sons and daughters since they joined the military. Again, the parents of these young men and women said the pictures alleviated a lot of their fears about the kinds of activities their children were involved in. The old saying that a picture is worth a thousand words is really true in this instance.

Servicemen and women transferring to the Norfolk-Virginia Beach area also checked out our activities on our website. The wife of one young naval officer who had orders to attend school at the Naval Air Station Oceana-Dam Neck Annex found our website on the Internet and contacted us. When they arrived, they immediately became a regular part of our fellowship.

A young woman in the Air Force who was looking for information about churches for a friend who was being transferred to Korea, sent us the following email after coming across our website:

"I am stationed at the AF Academy in Colorado Springs. What an awesome ministry you have!! That is pretty cool!! I was looking for a website for churches in Kunsan, Korea, when I came across your website. One of my friends is moving to Kunsan AB, and I am just looking at churches or ministries there for him to get involved in, and I thought you may know some people there.... I would appreciate all the help we can get."

Christian parents searching online for military ministries on behalf of their sons and daughters contacted us as well. We received the following email from the mother of a sailor stationed on a ship homeported at the Norfolk Naval Station:

"I just found your website and will be forwarding it to my son.... He is a sailor aboard the USS [ ].... He is living aboard the ship and is about to go nuts. Nowhere to relax, nowhere that is like a "home," nowhere to be alone. He goes to the mall every day after work, just to get off the ship.... Your "house church" sounds like something that might attract him. He is kind of shy, so I don't know if he will contact you or not. I think your outreach sounds so much like what he needs. He is lonely and my mother's heart is breaking for him.... He needs family.... I just wanted to give you a heads up, as I am praying that he will have the nerve to contact you."

In February 2008 we received an email from Rubem Carvalho, a young sailor in the Brazilian Navy. Living in Rio de Janeiro, he explained that while surfing the web to find information about Norfolk, Virginia, he came across our website. He said he attended an Assembly of God church in Rio, and that his ship was scheduled to be in Norfolk for four to six weeks for combined training exercises with the United States Navy. He asked if he could participate in our ministry activities while he was here.

I wrote back and said we would be delighted to have him join us! So, when the Brazilian ship *Fragata Greenhalgh* pulled into port at 8:00 Friday morning, June 13, 2008, Yvonne and I were at the pier to meet the ship.

After the ship tied up we were escorted on board and met Rubem and a friend of his named Rodrigo Santos (Camillo). We discovered Rubem could not speak English, and though Camillo could only speak a little bit, he would attempt to serve as our interpreter. We were able to make ourselves understood enough to make arrangements to come back at 6 o'clock that evening, after Rubem's work day ended, to bring him to our house for dinner.

When we came back, Rubem had four friends with him; Rodrigo (the young man we met earlier), and three others. Another friend of theirs, Daniel, had duty but joined us later for our weekend activities. They came to the house and joined us for dinner that evening—and every weekend after that while they were in port.

You Invited Me In...

Networking - Chaplains, Pastors and Commanding Officers

Sometimes our initial contact with servicemen and women is the result of networking with military chaplains, civilian pastors, and the commanding officers of military units. While Yvonne and I were attending the chapel at Little Creek Naval Amphibious Base, we met and developed a good working relationship with the commanding officer of the Marine Corps element at the Navy School of Music. He once had a female marine who was going through a difficult period of adjustment in her training. Contacting us, he asked if he could recommend that his Marine participate in our weekend activities as a means of providing some encouragement and support for her. We agreed wholeheartedly, and she became an active participant in our ministry. She even invited some friends from her unit to participate as well. Her mother sent us the following email:

"I wanted to take a couple of minutes to say thank you. My daughter...has just started attending your bible studies and get togethers. I spoke to her on the phone yesterday just as she was leaving your home to go back to the base. She has gone through a rough time the last 5-6 weeks, and I wanted to tell you she has not sounded more like herself since she left for boot camp last January than she did on the phone with me yesterday. There was a lightness to her voice and a joy and excitement I haven't heard in a very long time. I cried tears of joy when I hung up with her. It was like she...was back again. I know you do wonderful work...I went to the website today and to my wonderful surprise, there was a smiling, happy [daughter] with all of you and all of her new friends. She looks so comfortable and is just beaming! I look forward to meeting you when I am down for graduation next month. Thank you for becoming part of [her] military family!"

Making Contact

When this young marine musician graduated from the School of Music, Yvonne and I attended her graduation ceremony where we *did* meet her family. Her commanding officer expressed his appreciation for the help we gave his marine and his command.

Divine Intervention

At other times, making the initial contact with a serviceman is through a direct divine intervention. Let me share a story to illustrate what I mean. Several years ago, the associate pastor of Seaport Community Church (Assemblies of God) in Groton, Connecticut, near the Naval Submarine School, discovered our website and contacted us for help in developing an outreach ministry to the military.

At first, we assisted as much as possible through email discussions. Then we scheduled a trip to Connecticut to meet the pastor. During our visit, we took him to the chaplain's office and introduced him to one of the base chaplains. The pastor surprised the chaplain by asking how he could assist the chaplain in his efforts to minister to the sailors on his base.

The chaplain commented that he was the first pastor to ever offer his services like that, including pastors of his own denomination. The meeting forged an alliance between that chaplain and the pastor that led to several cooperative ministry efforts between them.

The submarine base in Groton has a beautiful chapel. So after our meeting with the chaplain, we went to see it. We had an "accidental" meeting with a young sailor—we all collided in the entry to the chapel. After we all assured each other that we were all right physically, we began talking and laughing about the incident.

As we talked, we had an opportunity to turn the conversation to spiritual things. We talked to the young sailor about his faith and about Jesus Christ. The pastor extended an invitation for the sailor to visit his church, which he accepted. He attended regularly, and within a few weeks, accepted Jesus Christ as his Savior. He stayed in touch with us as well, and described his new spiritual journey through a series of emails. In his first email, he said:

> "I am not sure if you remember me.... We met...outside [the Navy chapel] in Groton CT. I wish to thank you for that seemingly coincidental meeting. I, in the past several weeks and month have found God, well finding would be a better way to describe it. I have attended Seaport Community Church fairly diligently and [am] going to church with my sister when I visit her. I have also been growing as a Christian, trying to figure out what it means mainly. I am not sure you remember the details of that day, but I wish to thank you for being there. Pastor...gave me a link to your website the other day. I hope you can respond to me. God bless."

I did respond to him. And later he wrote and told me about his desire to read the Bible:

> "Of late I've been reading the Bible and other religious material.... One of my goals for this year is to try to read the entire Bible within a year, I only started beginning of January to have a plan. The Christian bookstore had a little planner thing and I bought a Bible I liked.... I have also been using your web page recently to learn more about different things in the Bible. Thank you for responding and being there."

He asked for prayer and talked about exploring our website:

> "[I] received the newsletter from you last week. Thank you very much. I have been praying that God would put me someplace that would help me grow in him and bring me joy. I also wish to ask for you to pray for me in the

next coming days or any advice you can give during the next several weeks. I also found your webpage to be immensely informative. Thank you again for being at the church that day. God bless."

Then he wrote about his experience sharing his personal testimony at a men's retreat weekend:

"One weekend me and fifty other men went on a retreat to encounter God. I must say it changed me greatly as I said in my testimony to around 200 people. The first thing I said...I hate speaking to large groups, even small groups give me pause. But I felt almost no fear and was the second to give [a] testimony... I...told how about a year ago I wanted to kill myself and almost committed suicide. I have not been water baptized yet, but was baptized by the holy spirit on Sunday in the afternoon.... I remember just a few months ago the way I felt about God and church and now they have radically changed. I thank you for being there that...day. God bless you!"

God orchestrated our steps that day and brought us into contact with a young sailor who was spiritually hungry and searching for meaning in his life.

NavyForMoms.com

Finally, Yvonne and I frequent a website called *NavyForMoms.com* that was developed to provide the mothers of young men and women who are in the Navy, or about to join the Navy, an online forum to meet, ask questions, and share information and experiences. As a retired Navy chaplain and a Navy wife, we joined the forum so we could be an encouragement to those moms, and especially for the ones who have sons or daughters stationed in the Hampton Roads area. During our online interaction with the moms, we let them know

You Invited Me In...

about our ministry, and that their sons or daughters would be welcome to participate in our activities if they want to. Many have sent us private messages and emails, asking us to contact their sons and daughters. We have also had moms recommend us to their sons and daughters, encouraging them to contact us.

So, you can see there are a variety of ways we make initial contact with the servicemen and women that we invite into our home. Not everyone accepts our invitation, and not all who come once, return. But we are here for them and our home is open to them. We continue praying for *every* serviceman and woman who comes into our home.

If you choose to open your home, God may lead you to contact the military men and women in your area in still other ways. Remember, it's God who establishes the connections.

6

YOU INVITED ME INTO YOUR LIVES

Making the initial contact with servicemen and women, and inviting them into our home is just the beginning. Getting them to actually come to the house for the first time is the next step. That often takes quite a bit of effort!

Yvonne texts or calls each soldier, sailor, or marine every week to find out if they are coming on Saturday evening or Sunday afternoon. This is how we let them know we are getting together for our activities, how we reassure them that we want them to join us, and helps Yvonne know how much food to buy and prepare for the weekend meals.

But, let me share a little secret with you: even when she calls or texts them, many don't let us know whether they are coming over or not until the very last minute. And sometimes, when they say they are coming over, they don't. Or they say they are not coming over, and suddenly show up at the front door.

Occasionally, the doorbell rings and we open the front door, and from the surprised look on our faces, they sheepishly explain, "My other plans fell through. Is it ok for me to join you?" Our answer is always, "Of course!" We never turn away a young serviceman or woman who wants to join us for our activities.

There have, however, been a few awkward moments when a serviceman showed up at the door when Yvonne and I thought no one was coming over, no food was prepared, and no activities were planned. I remember one particular Sunday afternoon a few years ago that has become one of our funny memories.

That Sunday, we thought no one was coming over, so Yvonne and I decided to kick back and relax. I joked with her saying, "Just because we're not planning anything, and you're not cooking, watch someone show up."

I turned around and looked out the front window. And sure enough, one of our sailors drove up and parked in front of the house. And not only did *he* get out of the car, he had invited another young couple from his church, too! They came to the front door, and we invited them in, but apologized that there was no meal prepared. The young sailor didn't miss a beat. He smiled really big and said, "Oh, that's ok! Do you have any peanut butter and jelly?" We all laughed, and that afternoon we entertained with peanut butter and jelly sandwiches. We even took pictures to prove it!

We've learned that it often takes several attempts to coax, or convince, these young people that they are truly welcome in our home, and that we *want* them to come over. And, just maybe, that what we are offering them is a better alternative than something else they were thinking about doing on Saturday night or Sunday afternoon. We try really hard to make sure all of the servicemen and women we contact know, when we invite them to come to our house, that they are welcome to join us *every* weekend if they want to.

A serviceman's schedule is frequently unpredictable. Personal plans and duty schedules can change suddenly and unexpectedly. One moment they can't come over and the next they can. So in this ministry, flexibility is essential!

You Invited Me Into Your Lives

Yvonne and I realize that the servicemen and women we make contact with may not necessarily want to come over when we invite them. There may be other things they choose to do besides coming to our house, eating hamburgers and playing board games. We know our activities are only *one* option among many things they can do.

We try to remember that the reason we do what we do is to minister to the soldier, sailor, and marine. If we make the ministry itself, or the number of servicemen or women who come over at any one time our focus, it would be easy to get discouraged. Our focus has to be on the individual young person and our relationship with them, regardless of the unpredictability of their schedules. The purpose and goal of all of our activities is about building redemptive relationships with the young military person who comes into our home whenever they can or whenever they want to.

In addition to their personal activities and work schedules, there may be a hesitancy on their part to accept our invitation simply because we are strangers. Most of these young people have been taught to be cautious around strangers. We live in a day when parents exercise great care to keep their children safe and protect them from strangers who might wish to harm them. They teach them not to speak to strangers, and not to accept rides from people they do not know. They hope to instill a healthy fear of strangers from the time they are small in the hope that doing so will keep them safe. Sometimes they continue cautioning them like this well into their late teen years, and even after they join the military.

Let me give you an example of what I mean. Not long after we started our ministry here, we were fellowshipping with the chaplains at Oceana Naval Air Station in Virginia Beach. The senior chaplain called me aside one day and cautioned me about inviting young sailors into our home.

You Invited Me In...

He said, "John, you've got to be really careful about inviting these sailors into your home, because you never know what kind of spirit they may bring in with them."

I replied, "Thank you for the warning. But I believe God told us to invite them in. We have to do what He told us to do. And I believe that if we are obedient to Him, He will protect us."

"O.K.," he said, "Just be careful."

A few months later, we tried for several weeks to convince a young sailor from Portsmouth Naval Medical Center to come over to the house and join us for our activities. She seemed interested, but always had some "reason" why she could not come. Finally, she accepted our invitation, and enjoyed herself at one of our Saturday evening activity nights. At the end of the evening, we were all sitting in the living room talking and getting to know each other, when she explained her hesitation about coming over.

She said, "I told my mom about you guys, and that I was thinking about coming to your house and joining you for your activities."

Mom said, "Be really careful! Because you don't know what kind of people they are. And you don't know what they might do to you."

Immediately, my mind went back to the chaplain's warning, and I thought how ironic these two situations were. The chaplain saw danger in our inviting servicemen and women into our home, and the sailor's mother saw danger in her daughter accepting our invitation. I shared the story of the chaplain's warning with her. All of us saw the humor in the irony and laughed.

There are also young adults who are just shy by nature, and reluctant to come into a stranger's home. Recall the email I shared earlier from the mother of a sailor who said she found our website and forwarded the information to her son. She said he was living onboard his ship and was "about to go nuts." He

You Invited Me Into Your Lives

would go to the mall every day after work just to get off the ship. She also shared that he was "kind of shy," so wasn't sure if he would contact us or not. He was lonely and her mother's heart was breaking for him. But in spite of this young man's loneliness and frustration, he never did contact us.

Trying to minister to young servicemen and women is a lot like fishing. When Jesus called His disciples, He said, *"Follow me, and I will make you fishers of men."*[38] When you go fishing, you throw your line into the water and wait. For us, that's the initial contact.

After a while you might see the bobber move, or bounce. That's the fish touching or nibbling on the bait. Again, for us, that would be the serviceman or woman showing interest in our activities.

Then maybe, if you're patient, the bobber goes under the water. That may be the fish grabbing the bait. But there's no guarantee you've caught the fish. In our analogy, that's the serviceman or woman accepting our invitation.

Finally, when you see the bobber go under the water and stay there, you've hooked the fish. For us, that's when the young military man or woman actually comes over to the house, walks through the door, and becomes part of our family.

After making the initial contact with service members, inviting them to our home, and after they've actually walked through our front door for the first time, Yvonne and I try hard to make them feel like they are part of a real family. We even tell them, as I've said before, that they are "guests" in our home only the first time they come over. After that, if they decide to come back, we "adopt" them and they become part of our family.

Yvonne and I are "huggers." So the young men and women who come into our home get hugged a lot. It's our way of showing love. Some like it and some don't. If a serviceman or

---

[38] Matthew 4:19, ESV

woman really doesn't like it, we won't hug them. But very few have ever not wanted to be included in our "gauntlet" when they come in or go out our front door.

Several years ago, we had a young sailor come to the house who was of Japanese descent and was clearly not accustomed to hugging. He let us hug him, but he would almost stand at attention, really stiff and uncomfortable at first. As time went on, he began to hug us back, and actually seemed to enjoy the hugs. Just before going home on Christmas leave, he said, "When I get home I'm going to try hugging my father." When he got back I asked him how that went. He looked down sadly and said, "Not very well." Eventually, it came time for him to transfer to another duty station. But before he left he said, "You know what I think I'm going to miss the most? Your big bear hugs!"

Pictures, Pictures, and More Pictures

Photography has been my hobby since I was a young sailor and bought my first "fancy" camera. So pictures are a big part of our ministry. We take lots of them! And what proud parent or grandparent doesn't display hundreds of pictures of their sons and daughters and grandchildren?

The same is true for us. Our fireplace mantle is full of pictures of the soldiers, sailors, and marines who have been through our home. Many of them have now been away from here for years, but they still send us pictures of themselves and their families at Christmas. Some have gotten married and started families of their own, so more and more of the pictures they send us include their new spouses and babies. It's fun to watch our extended "family" grow!

We also put a lot of pictures of the servicemen and women involved in our activities on our website and weekly blog. People who are interested in our ministry, and who come to our website or blog, see what we do as well as read about our activities. The pictures let the servicemen see themselves from any computer in the world, so they can feel like they are still connected to us even when they go on deployment or get transferred to another duty station.

So you can see, that once we meet a young serviceman or woman it takes intentionality and effort to get them to come into our home. Yvonne and I believe providing a comfortable home and family environment and regularly scheduled social activities makes the development of close personal relationships with these young men and women possible. These close personal relationships then provide us with opportunities to share the Gospel of Jesus Christ with them. In the following section I want to describe in detail what we do in our activities.

Saturday Evening 5:00 – 9:00 PM

Relationships takes time to build. So we try to spend as much time together as possible. Our activities start every Saturday afternoon at 5 o'clock. We meet at our house, where the fun starts with eating together: usually hot dogs, hamburgers, tacos, or pizzas.

After we eat, about 6 o'clock, we start the games. We play lots of board games: Monopoly, Clue, Risk, Settlers of Catan, Phase Ten, Uno Attack, and many, many others. Sometimes we have a movie night and watch Christian DVDs. Other times we go bowling, or miniature golfing. Our activities end at 9 o'clock.

But before they do, we go into the living room, share prayer requests and pray together. For some, sharing prayer requests and praying is strange and takes some getting used to.

Special Event Activities

For many years we took our group to see the Ringling Brothers Barnum and Bailey Circus when it came to town. One year we had some servicemen and women with us who had never been to a circus. It was as much fun watching them react to the

You Invited Me In...

excitement, color, and pageantry of a three-ring circus as it was to watch the circus itself!

An hour before the circus started we would go down to the arena and take pictures with the clowns and other performers. That was always a highlight of the evening for me.

During baseball season, we go to watch a Norfolk Tides baseball game. The Norfolk Tides are a minor league baseball team affiliated with the Baltimore Orioles, and play at the Norfolk Harbor Park field. In 2008, we took the Brazilian sailors to their first ever American baseball game. It was great fun! I had to explain some of the basics of the game, so they could understand what was happening on the field, but they really enjoyed it. And again, we took lots of pictures.

In recent years, the military community in Norfolk has hosted an International Tattoo. This is one of the newer events we attend. Military bands from the United States and many foreign countries perform. The dazzling, vibrant colors of the uniforms, the exhilarating sound of the music, and the inspiring pageantry of the bands as they play and drill are awesome!

Sometimes, our Saturday activities are day trips. Every year, we attend the Civil War re-enactment in Yorktown, Virginia. Afterward, we eat pizza at a local Italian restaurant, followed by ice cream for dessert at a local ice cream parlor.

Near us are Historic Yorktown, Williamsburg and the Jamestown Plantation that we make day trips to see. We've even been involved in a mock 1774 trial in Williamsburg and been sentenced to the "stocks" for preaching the Gospel without the proper license!

On several occasions, we've gone to the Outer Banks of North Carolina where we climbed the 220 steps to the top of Currituck Beach Lighthouse. We've eaten custom made Duck Donuts in Duck, North Carolina. And we've visited the Wright Brothers' Museum in Kitty Hawk, posing for some fun pictures at the bronze replica of the original Wright Brothers Flyer.

You Invited Me Into Your Lives

What Makes Our Saturday Activities Meaningful?

As part of the research for my doctorate several years ago, I wanted to know how the servicemen and women involved in our ministry felt about what we did. I developed a survey that I sent to 116 of them. Forty-six completed the survey. This was only a snapshot in time, but I was very pleased and encouraged by the feedback I received.

One of the things I wondered about was just how significant our Saturday afternoon activities were to the young people who came to our home. So in my survey I asked them specifically what made our Saturday activities special to them. I've included some of their responses:

One young sailor said, "I remember the laughs, and the jokes."

The wife of a sailor said, "I love playing board games!"

Another sailor commented, "It was nice having something to do with people that didn't involve a lot of drinking."

A marine said, "I didn't feel pressure to sin."

A young sailor from Colorado said, "It was nice speaking with other service members without the constant foul communication."

And finally, a female soldier said, "John and Yvonne were wonderful "parents" for me during my stay in Virginia."

Yvonne and I were encouraged by their comments. And we realized that our Saturday family activities really did matter to the young men and women who had become part of our family.

Sunday Afternoon 1:00 to 5:00 PM

Then it's on to our Sunday activities. Sundays start at 6 o'clock in the morning for Yvonne. She starts her day cooking the noon meal. One of her specialties is homemade bread. Everybody loves it! She's even taught a few of the girls and guys how to bake their own bread.

You Invited Me In...

Then, while the bread is baking, she starts in on the desserts. One of my favorites is her cheese cake. OK, the decadent chocolate Bundt cake is awesome, too! As I write, images are floating around in my head of big pieces of cake filled with chocolate chips, chocolate frosting, drizzled with white chocolate, and covered in dark chocolate chunks. But then there's her mom's German apple crisp...Well, I think you get the idea!

Yvonne's bread and dessert creations are followed by the main courses that include the meat and potatoes. She prepares delicious pot roasts, meat loafs, pork tenderloins, fried chicken, and spaghetti with homemade sauce.

Her vegetables are special too. A lot of young people come here and say, "I don't eat vegetables!" Or, "I don't eat anything green!" Yvonne coaxes them to try her garlic laced green beans. She's made some diehard vegetable haters into vegetable eaters!

Watching Yvonne at work in the kitchen on Sunday morning is like watching the conductor of a symphony orchestra. I could never keep all those things going at the same time without burning something.

About 1 o'clock, everyone starts arriving. While Yvonne puts the finishing touches on dinner, some pitch in and help her cook. Others sit around enjoying the fellowship and getting to know each other. Still others play games on their phones.

We sit down at the dining room table about 2 o'clock to eat dinner "family style." And there's always enough food! Even when someone rings the door bell and says, "I brought a couple of my friends. I hope its O.K." We tell the new ones who come over, "If you leave our table hungry, it's your own fault!"

After dinner, we go into the living room and watch Christian DVDs or Bible videos, football games, or just talk and get to know each other. A lot of times, we share family stories, talk about high school or college days, our military experiences, our brothers and sisters, or our church and religious backgrounds.

Whenever there are new service members, we go around the room and take turns reading a gospel tract entitled, "Have You Heard of the Four Spiritual Laws?"[39]

Our Sunday afternoons conclude with going around the room sharing prayer requests, and praying for each other. For many, sharing prayer requests and praying together is a whole new experience.

Our activities usually end about 5 o'clock; but some of the guys don't like to leave that early, and just hang out here until six, seven, or even eight o'clock at night.

What Makes Our Sunday Activities Meaningful?

As with our Saturday-night activities, I also wanted to know how meaningful the things we did on Sunday afternoons were to those who participated in them, and what made them so. Here again are a few of the responses I received:

A young female soldier said, "I really enjoyed those Sunday dinners, because they were much like the dinners we had with my family at home. They were special because I felt very welcomed and enjoyed the togetherness that the atmosphere of your home created."

A sailor said, "The feeling of family I received made the world of difference!"

A soldier's wife made the comment, "It reminded me of home, being with friends and family around the dinner table."

A female marine from Nevada explained, "My family back home ate at 2 o'clock on the weekends and we all sat around the dinner table and talked about our week....being able to still do that while being away from everything that is familiar is very comforting."

---

[39] This is a small pamphlet that is a very clear, easy to understand, presentation of the Gospel message.

You Invited Me In...

A female sailor said, "I liked that I got to help. It helped me not to have to be so uptight. I knew I could relax."

While another sailor commented, "It was nice to have a dinner away from the military environment, with a family."

And finally, a soldier said, "Just spending time with fellow Christians was great....like being at home with loving parents."

The sentiments expressed were again really encouraging! They showed us that what we were doing made a difference in the lives of these young people who were so far away from their own families.

That's what our weekends are like. Every weekend! Fun, food, family, fellowship, and faith. But that's just where things get started. Let me share some of our family traditions and stories that go beyond the regular weekend activities.

Birthday Celebrations

We keep track of our sons' and daughters' birthdays. Yvonne always asks if they have a favorite meal or dessert. Then she prepares it for them on the weekend nearest their special day. She buys little gifts for them too just to let them know that they are remembered and special.

Holiday Traditions

Many people think our busiest days are during the Thanksgiving and Christmas holiday season. But they are not. Because that's when most of our soldiers, sailors, and marines go home on leave to their real families.

But there are usually a few who can't go home. So Yvonne does the same thing for them on Thanksgiving, Christmas, and Easter that she does on Sunday mornings. Except during the holidays there is more food and more elaborate decorations. Did I say *more* food?

On Thanksgiving we always have the traditional Thanksgiving turkey with all of the trimmings. Sometimes, if the

You Invited Me Into Your Lives

people who come over have special side dishes they like, Yvonne prepares them.

Since Yvonne and I are German, during the Christmas season we bring out a lot of our German family traditions. For instance, we always have a *real* Christmas tree, with *real* candles, that we *really* light! It's a German Christmas tradition attributed to Martin Luther. He was supposed to have said that the evergreen tree represented eternal life, and that the candles represented Jesus as the light of the world.

We try to have a Christmas party for everyone—with presents and everything—before they go home for the holidays. And since Christmas is actually the celebration of Jesus' birthday, Yvonne bakes a birthday cake for Jesus and we sing "Happy Birthday" to Him.

For Easter, Yvonne makes a roast leg of lamb for dinner. The lamb is symbolic of Jesus being "the Lamb of God who takes away the sins of the world."[40]

And finally, another tradition that we celebrate, though not German, is our annual St. Patrick's Day feast. That consists of corned beef and cabbage, boiled potatoes and carrots and Irish soda bread.

Family Stories

Our story wouldn't be complete without telling about some of the funny things that have happened over the years. The first one that comes to mind is about Yvonne's "croissants." Yvonne always makes homemade bread, which all the guys love! She also makes croissants.

One year we ran out of homemade bread, but had some leftover croissants in the freezer that she had from a previous dinner. So she pulled them out and put them on a paper plate. She sprinkled some water on them, covered them with a paper

---

[40] John 1:29, ESV.

towel, and put them in the microwave for a few seconds to thaw and warm. When they were ready, she took the paper towel off the plate and brought them to the table. I watched with horror what happened from the far end of the table where I was sitting.

The first person helped himself to a croissant and passed the basket of rolls to the person seated next to him. The first guy took a bite, and enjoyed it. The next person took a croissant and passed the basket on. He had to exert a bit more effort to bite into it. The third person took one and when he tried to take a bite of his roll, gave up and quietly put the croissant down on his plate without finishing it. My eyes widened when I watched the next sailor take a croissant, which was really hard by now, and actually BANG! it on the table. You get the picture.

The following week, one of the sailors asked Yvonne if she had any more of those "delicious" croissants, and grinned. The week after that another sailor asked the same question. They started saying Yvonne's croissants would make good bullets if we ever ran out of ammunition in a war. Or, filled with gun powder, they would make good depth charges. Yvonne took the good-natured teasing really well! But after a while, I tried to get them to stop, to no avail.

Yvonne studied sign language and had a dictionary of sign language vocabulary words. The guys asked her what the sign for "croissant" was, and then asked what the sign for "queen" was. Once they learned those two signs, they didn't say anything about the croissants anymore. They just signed "croissant queen." Years later, those who were here, still tease her about it. Sometimes in a P.S. in an email, or in a comment on Facebook, they'll ask her if she's made any more of her "delicious croissants."

Then there is the story about the Virginia Christmas ham. We usually have ham for Christmas dinner. But ever since moving to Virginia, I've wanted to try a Virginia ham to see what the difference was between that and a regular ham. So, one year, Yvonne bought a dry-cured, Virginia ham for Christmas. Not knowing what the difference was, we read the directions, which said if we wanted a less salty taste to soak the ham in water for six to eight hours. But, I like a salty tasting ham, rather than the sweet, honey-glazed ham taste. So I said, "No, let's not soak it. We'll just fix it the way we fix a normal ham."

We put it on a rack in the oven and roasted it. A few hours later, it was time to eat. Everything was ready. Everyone was gathered around the table. And I took the ham out of the oven. But it looked really strange! It looked all dried out, and had salt crystals all over it. And it smelled weird too. Well, I found out later that the smell of a Virginia ham is different than a normal ham, so that was really not a problem.

But when I tasted the meat, it was incredibly salty, even for me! It tasted really bad, not like any ham I had ever eaten before. I didn't like it at all, and wondered what I was going to do. I had guests at the table, waiting for dinner. So I went ahead and sliced the ham, and put it on a platter. There was no moisture in that piece of meat at all! I got it to the table, and we said grace. Everyone helped themselves, and we began eating.

After a few bites, I couldn't eat it any more. I could see from the looks on almost everyone's faces that they were not enjoying it, either. That is, all except one sailor. I acknowledged to everyone that it was horrible, and told them they did not have to finish it. They could just leave the ham. But this one sailor actually went back for seconds. I told him he didn't have to do that. Then he went back for thirds! Again, I said he didn't have to eat it. It would not hurt our feelings if he didn't.

But he said, "No, it's O.K. I like it." His fiancé was sitting next to him, and we all watched him eat this meat that was more like a salt lick than a ham. He seemed to be sincerely enjoying it. That wasn't the best Christmas dinner we ever had, by far!

Several months later, on Easter Sunday, we were all gathered around the dinner table again. Most of the same people were

You Invited Me In...

there who ate Christmas dinner with us. Yvonne cooked a leg of lamb and a pot roast. The pot roast was just in case some didn't like lamb.

During the meal, I asked the young man who had eaten the Christmas ham to pass me the salt shaker. He didn't hear me, so the young lady sitting next to him, now his wife, elbowed him and said,

"Pass the salt to John."

He was startled and said, "No thanks, I haven't needed any salt since Christmas!"

Everyone at the table broke out laughing!

Other Relationship-Building Opportunities

Many of the young men and women who have participated in our activities were in the Norfolk-Virginia Beach area attending specialized schools to prepare them for their military jobs. These students were not allowed to have cars, so we picked them up at their barracks, brought them to the house, and following our activities took them back to their bases. It's amazing how much "relationship building" happened in the car during those trips.

The service schools these young men and women attend hold graduation ceremonies for their students. And like any good "parent," we support and encourage our adopted sons and daughters by attending them.

As a minister I perform weddings, water baptisms, and funerals as a regular part of my ministerial duties. And in the normal course of life, some of the men and women who have been part of our fellowship have gotten married. Their weddings are usually held in their home states. And, if at all possible, Yvonne and I travel to those states to attend, participate in, or officiate at the weddings. It's exciting to be included as part of these significant milestones in our adopted sons' and daughters' lives!

Undoubtedly the most unusual wedding I performed was for one of our sailors who was very active in theater. His wedding had a "pirate" theme where he, the bridesmaids, and the groomsmen were all dressed in pirate costumes that he had custom-made by a tailor in Bahrain. He asked me to perform the wedding in costume, and asked Yvonne to stand in for his mother, also in costume. We agreed, and had our costumes made locally. Then we drove to Oregon to perform the wedding. People said I looked like Benjamin Franklin and Yvonne looked like Betsy Ross.

When we got to Oregon, the bride-to-be asked if I would baptize her in water the day before the wedding. It was an unusual request, so I sat and talked with her about the meaning of water baptism. She assured me that she had accepted Jesus Christ as her Savior, but had never been baptized in water, and wanted to do that for her new husband. So on the day before the wedding, both the bride and the groom's families and Yvonne and I drove to the Columbia River and held a water baptismal service on a beautiful, sunny, summer day!

Sometimes during the year, parents and siblings of the servicemen and women who come over to the house, come to the Norfolk-Virginia Beach area to visit their sons and daughters. If they let us know ahead of time, Yvonne and I like to extend an invitation for them to stay with us, instead of at a local motel. Hosting a serviceman or woman's extended family is always fun because it lets us build relationships with them. Often, during their visit they participate in our weekend activities which gives them a direct, firsthand view of what we do in our ministry.

All of these activities, events, and celebrations are the way we build relationships with young military men and women and their families. There is a great deal of satisfaction that comes with getting to know them at this early stage in their adult lives.

You Invited Me In...

And it gives Yvonne and me a real sense of fulfillment as we share our lives with them, and they share their lives with us.

Ministry Challenges

While hospitality house military ministry is vital and necessary, it is not without significant challenges. Developing relationships with young military men and women can be difficult even when the ministry is focused specifically on them.

For most service members, a normal tour of duty can vary anywhere from a few weeks at a military school, to several years on an Army, Navy, Marine Corps, or Air Force base. Schedules are hectic, erratic, uncertain, subject to change without notice, and often "classified" for national security reasons. During their tour of duty in an area, they will have "duty days" and "duty weekends" where they are restricted to their ships or posts to stand a variety of watches.

Because of their erratic schedules, a sailor will often come over to the house once or twice—and then disappear for days (or weeks) at a time—then suddenly pop back in again. They may come over one weekend and have duty the next. Sometimes, because of their limited free time, they choose to only come over one day during the weekend, or come one weekend and do something else the next. Then there are lengthy deployment schedules that keep them out of the area and out of ministry activities for months at a time.

Added to these military related schedules are the service members' personal leave periods, when they go home, and are out of the area for days or weeks again. Those with longer tours of duty can have those tours abruptly ended with little or no warning, suddenly getting transferred out of the area permanently. All of these scheduling issues makes spending time with them to develop relationships challenging.

Building relationships with young men and women serving in the military can be difficult because of these scheduling issues. But it can also be difficult because of their newfound freedom from parental influence. For instance, while they may miss their families, who may be hundreds or thousands of miles away, the distance does give them many new liberties. Mom and dad and the rest of the family are not constantly looking over their shoulders, monitoring their daily activities. They can come and go as they please and do things they might not do at home.

Young men and women who were raised in church now have the freedom to go to church or not, as they please. They will make new friends in their military units from other parts of the country and from very different cultural and religious backgrounds. These new friends may have very different moral, ethical, and behavioral standards from the ones they were raised with, and can have a profound influence on the newly "liberated" Christian young person.

For many, Yvonne and I become a "surrogate" parental influence. So, on one hand, our ministry is comforting for them because we provide a sense of family and love. But on the other, we represent the "parental influence" from which they recently liberated themselves.

As Christians Yvonne and I want to have a godly influence in their lives. But because of that, we also represent God and the church to them. As a result, they often *want* to participate in our activities and receive what we offer. But at the same time, may want to avoid us for the same reasons. All of this adds to the challenge we face in developing personal relationships with these young people.

Yvonne and I have learned over the years that in order to have a relationship with a service member, we have to pursue him or her and work to initiate the relationship. We have to make regular, intentional, and concerted efforts to stay engaged in his or her life. Military duties will always take precedence, and when it comes to free time, our ministry activities will also be in competition with every other activity these young adults and their new friends have available to them.

Let me go back to my earlier fishing analogy for a minute. If trying to get a serviceman or woman to come over to our house initially is like using a fishing line with a hook and bobber, then getting them to continue coming over, so a relationship can be established with them, is like trout fishing. Once you get a trout on the line and set the hook, reeling it in requires maintaining just the right tension on the line, gradually drawing it in and then letting the line out and allowing it to "run;" then reeling it in again.

Here again, if I had to select a few words to describe the skills needed by someone interested in ministering to the military in a hospitality house setting, they would be *flexibility, persistence* and *patience*!

This is why we feel that simply "honoring" the military in a special church service once or twice a year, and maybe even hosting a dinner in their honor afterward, is nice, but is simply not enough. These young adults need to know they are wanted, and that there is a consistency and regularity in any ministry that reaches out to them. They need to know that if they risk getting involved, but can't be there consistently—or if they go on deployment—they won't be forgotten. And, it is important for them to know that when their schedules allow them to come back they will be welcome, and that they will still have something to come back to.

I want to make sure I present an accurate and clear picture of this ministry. Hospitality house military ministry is challenging. It begins with making an initial contact with servicemen and women and inviting them to come over to the house to participate in planned activities. Some accept the invitation right away, and some do not. We don't give up after one invitation; we re-invite several times. Many young men and women get involved after receiving these repeated invitations.

Some, after coming to the house once or twice, choose not to come back. But again, we continue contacting them until it becomes obvious they are not interested in coming over any more. And finally, Yvonne and I have learned to accept the fact that not every serviceman or woman who comes into our home will develop a close personal relationship with us, or with the others who are involved in our ministry.

Attendance in our weekend and special events activities can vary dramatically from week to week. We've had as many as 17 sailors, soldiers, and marines around our table for a Sunday dinner, and then other weeks, we have had only one or two. The "success" of many Christian churches and ministries is measured by the number of people they have coming to a particular event at any given time. If the numbers are too low, the group may not be considered a viable ministry. But that can't be the criteria for a Pentecostal hospitality house military ministry. The focus in this style of ministry cannot be on "how many," but on the development of relationships with those who do come, whether that's one or 20.

Having said that, I admit that much of what we do is more fun when there are more people involved. That's true for Yvonne and me, and for the servicemen and women that come over as well. When there are more people, the atmosphere is alive and festive, like a big party. Truthfully, it's hard not to be disappointed when we go from 12 people one week to two people the next week. But it isn't always about a "party" atmosphere. Yvonne and I have had to learn that the one person that shows up may be in need of some personal attention— of some personal care. God may have sent that one young man or woman, on that particular day, knowing and intending that he or she would be the only one there.

Let me share a story with you to illustrate my point. One year we were planning for Thanksgiving dinner. Most of our regulars were going home for the holiday—all except one young soldier

You Invited Me In...

from the School of Music. He was new to our fellowship, and had only been to the house twice. He told us he was not going home for Thanksgiving, and when Yvonne invited him to join us, he said he would like that.

That year, we were also contacted by a Coast Guard cutter in the area who had a large group of sailors who had nowhere to go for Thanksgiving dinner. We sent word to the ship that their people were very welcome to come to our home and join us. They told us they had about 20 to 30 people who needed a place to go. Eleven sailors from their crew eventually committed to come. That was going to be a nice size crowd for us, so we were pretty excited!

Yvonne planned the menu, bought the groceries, did all the cooking and made all of the other preparations for the day. Thanksgiving Day came and the soldier from the School of Music arrived. Yvonne put the finishing touches on the meal and set the food on the table. And then we waited...and waited...and waited. It became apparent that no one from the Coast Guard cutter was coming. No one even called to let us know they were not coming. Yvonne and I were disappointed!

But we knew immediately that we couldn't let our disappointment overwhelm us, or we would ruin Thanksgiving dinner for the one young soldier who did show up. It was awkward at first, but then we joked around about it, and laughed about how much food we were all going to have to eat, and that we would be eating leftovers for months!

Dinner was fun, and filling! The soldier was a pleasant, quiet young man. And since he had only been to the house twice before; during dinner we shared family stories, and just got to know each other. After dinner, it was time for football; we watched two games during the afternoon.

During the course of the afternoon's conversation, we talked about our religious backgrounds and beliefs. His and mine were very similar; we had both been raised Lutheran. I shared my testimony with him, telling him how I came to know Jesus Christ as my Savior. Then we read through the *Have You Heard of the Four Spiritual Laws* gospel tract together.

I asked him if he had ever invited Jesus Christ into his life. He said, "No." And when I asked him if he would like to invite Christ into his life he said, "Yes, I would." Just to be sure he was talking about inviting Christ into his life right there, I asked him, "Is there anything that would keep you from doing that right now?" He simply said, "No, I guess not." So we prayed together, and he invited Jesus Christ into his heart to be his Savior and Lord.

I believe, that if there were a dozen people there, we probably would not have had that conversation. And had there been a dozen other people in the house, he probably would not have prayed that prayer. God knew who would be there that day. And He knew what that young soldier needed.

It would have been easy for Yvonne and me to focus on the Coast Guard crew that didn't show up. And it would have been easy to be angry because the leader of that group didn't even call to let us know they were not coming. But all of that would have taken away from the joy of the miracle that happened in our living room that day: a young soldier entering the kingdom of God! And that is what hospitality house military ministry is all about. That's why it can't just be about the "how many?" It has to be about relationships that change the eternal destinies of young military men and women.

The father of a young sailor sent us an email expressing his appreciation for the "family" relationships we were providing for his son. The father, who was himself a petty officer serving in the Naval Reserves, wrote:

> "I just have a moment, but I feel I have to drop you a
> note of thanks and gratitude for all you did, and
> continue to do for [my son]. I know for a fact that you

will always be in his heart. I know you will always be in mine as well.

"When our children grow up and head out into life we always worry about their wellbeing, and the transition to adult hood. The Lord brought you to him and for that I will be eternally grateful.

"I have heard you comment on how you wish you could reach a few more of our young sailors. Well I am here to say that it is not quantity but quality. I will never forget how you took in my son and helped him in his walk with the Lord....

"God bless all that you do for our children. Be it one or a hundred."

We hosted this father when he came to visit his son. During the visit he said he wanted to be "saved" like his son had been. So, while sitting in our kitchen, we helped the father of that young sailor invite Jesus Christ into his life.

Our Philosophy of Ministry

The Apostle Paul expressed our philosophy of ministry beautifully when in 1 Thessalonians 2:6-7, he said,

As apostles of Christ we could have been a burden to you, but we were gentle among you, like a <u>mother</u> caring for her little children...

And in 1 Thessalonians 2:11-12, where he said,

For you know that we dealt with each of you as a <u>father</u> deals with his own children, encouraging, comforting

and urging you to live lives worthy of God, who calls you into his kingdom and glory...

And in 1 Thessalonians 2:8, where he summarized our heart attitude about these servicemen and women,

We loved you so much that we were delighted to share with you not only the gospel of God but <u>our lives</u> as well, because you had become so dear to us.

Yvonne and I believe that couples—and individuals—with a love for young adults, and the military in particular, can open their homes to one or two service members and create a place for them in their family. We're sharing our story with you so that some of you who read it may catch the vision and say, "Hey, I can do that!"

And by the way, the "numbers" do eventually add up. Over the years, the cumulative number of people the Lord uses you to reach increases! They just don't all show up in your living room on the same day. The relationships you build with these young people can, and often do, last for years and even a lifetime!

As our sons and daughters began transferring to other places, they wrote to us and said they missed us and our fellowship. They asked if we knew of anyone in their new area who was doing the same thing we were. But we didn't.

There are young military men and women all over the country, and we know we can't reach them all, or be in every place at the same time. So, we began praying that the Lord would raise up workers and send them into His harvest field to reach military men and women all over the country.

7

YOU SHARED JESUS WITH ME

In 2001, Yvonne and I began attending the Naval Air Station Oceana Dam Neck Annex chapel on Sunday mornings. There we met a young eighteen-year-old sailor who we invited to our home several times to participate in our activities. But each time he said he was "busy," or had other things to do. Then suddenly, one week he asked us if we could meet during the week at a restaurant near the base to have a cup of coffee. We were surprised by his request; but agreed, and suggested we meet for dinner instead of just coffee. While we ate, we talked about our lives, and our families, and just got to know each other. After a while the conversation turned to spiritual things, and we talked about God, our faith, and our church backgrounds.

At one point Yvonne asked him if he had ever heard of the four spiritual laws? He said, "No." So she explained that, just like there are physical laws that govern the physical universe, there are spiritual laws that govern our relationship with God. She told him that God loved him and had a wonderful plan for his life. But, because of the sin in his life, he was separated from God and couldn't know or experience God's love or His plan for his life. She told him that Jesus Christ was God's only way of dealing with his sin — and that to experience God's love and plan for his life, he needed to turn from his sin and receive Jesus Christ as his Savior. Then she shared a simple prayer that he could pray if he wanted to invite Jesus into his heart and life.

Yvonne asked him if he had ever prayed a prayer like that, or invited Jesus into his life. Again he said, "No."

So she asked him if he would like to do that. He said, "Yes, he would."

She suggested we all bow our heads and pray together. He looked surprised, glanced around the room nervously, and became somewhat reluctant.

He whispered, "But this is such a public place!"

Yvonne agreed, but said, "Jesus died on the cross for you in a public place, too, in plain sight of everyone."

After he thought for a moment, he said, "Ok, let's do it." He bowed his head, and invited Jesus Christ into his life.

This is what our ministry is all about: introducing young men and women to Jesus Christ—helping them invite Christ into their hearts and lives so they can know and experience God's love and plan for their lives. This, however, is by no means the end of the story. It is only the beginning—the beginning of a whole new life for men and women like this young sailor.

So far in this book, I've talked about providing a safe, comfortable, home and family environment for servicemen and women—having regularly-scheduled, enjoyable social activities in that environment to prepare the way for establishing close personal relationships. Then together, the home environment, the social activities, and the personal relationships increase their willingness to listen to the presentation of the gospel message.

In this and the next three chapters, I want to explain what we do when we present the Full Gospel message of salvation. I want to share how we present a Christ-centered message to the young military men and women who come into our home. And I want share some of the results of presenting that message over the past 18 years.

Our hope is that you will see how important a Christ-centered message is; and what God has allowed us to accomplish in the lives of these young men and women right in our living room. And hopefully, you will see how you can achieve the same kind of results in your home.

Our Words Are Important

Let me begin by saying that the gospel message is all about words. Words that have been conveyed from God, through the human beings who wrote the Bible, to us today.

Words are important. I can't emphasize that enough! We communicate with each other using words. The words we use have meaning. With them we convey concepts, ideas, and beliefs. We use words when we discuss questions like, "What is truth?" and "What is reality?" and "What is the meaning of life?"

We formulate our beliefs and attitudes from the words we hear, the words we think about, and the words we use. Words are important because what we believe to be true, and what we believe is real, affects the decisions we make, and ultimately our behavior.

Let me give you an example. Let's say a young woman gets pregnant unexpectedly. What she believes about the cells that are growing in her body will affect her decisions and actions toward those cells. If she believes those cells are a baby, and that that baby has a right to live, she will make the decision to carry that baby to term, give birth and raise the child—or make arrangements for someone else to raise it.

However, if she believes those cells are simply a mass of tissue, similar to an unwanted tumor, she may decide to have it surgically removed. Even if she believes those cells will eventually become a baby, if she believes she has the right to do whatever she wants to with her body, and if being pregnant at that particular time is inconvenient for her, she may decide to end her pregnancy by having an abortion. So you can see, what a young woman believes affects her decisions; and those decisions ultimately affect her behavior.

Words also communicate beliefs and ideas about God. And what a person believes, or does not believe, about God, will also affect that person's decisions and behavior. However, what a person believes about God goes beyond simply affecting their behavior in this life. The things a person believes are true and real about God impact their eternal destiny.

Let me offer another example. Assume for a moment that the words in the Bible are true, and the God of the Bible is real. According to the words in the Bible, if a young man believes in Jesus Christ, and in what Jesus did on the Cross, and has asked Him for forgiveness for his sins and invited Him into his heart, when that young man dies he will go to heaven. If, on the other hand, he chooses not to believe in Jesus Christ, he will spend eternity in hell.

If, however, the words in the Bible are just stories made up by a particular group of religious people, and the God of the Bible is not real, then what that young man believes does not really matter. What he believes about Jesus Christ has no real effect on his eternal destiny.

Postmodernism is a mindset, the philosophical system that seriously impacts everyone, including most young adults today. According to it none of what I have just said, and none of what you and I believe, is really true.

According to postmodernism, there is nothing real behind any of our words. The words in the Bible about God and Jesus Christ are simply symbols that convey a particular set of ideas and beliefs held by a certain group of people, but nothing more. The God that those symbols describe is not really real. He is just a character in a story made up by religious people in a particular religious community. The people in that community may believe the words in the Bible, and they may believe the God of the Bible is real, but *in reality*, he is not. He only exists in the imagination of the people in the communities that choose to believe in him.

So according to this philosophical system, the God of the Bible is no more real than Santa Claus or the tooth fairy. The stories in the Bible are simply religious fairy tales. And, since the stories in the Bible are not describing reality, then the stories about heaven and hell are not describing real places, either.

When the young man in our example dies, he will simply be dead—nothing more, and nothing less. So while he is alive, he can believe in the teachings of Jesus Christ if he wants to. Or he can believe the teachings of Allah, Buddha, or no god at all. It doesn't really matter, because all religious beliefs are simply made up and not really real.

Because of the impact of this philosophical system, study after study shows that as many as 80 percent of young adults between the ages of 18 and 30 are indifferent to faith, God, and religion. They have been convinced that faith in God simply does not matter—because God is not real.

Postmodern philosophers go so far as to say that if these beliefs, or superstitions, were discarded completely, many of the difficulties in our global societies would disappear and everyone would get along much better, and be much happier. But until that happens, and since there is no reality behind any religious beliefs anyway, all of them should be considered equally true and valid, even if they totally contradict each other. Since these beliefs are only stories, and do not reflect reality, we should all come to the place where we accept one another's religious beliefs, regardless of what they are.

But postmodern philosophers go even further. They argue that it is actually an act of violence against another person to say that anything he or she believes is wrong. It therefore becomes socially unacceptable, and even morally wrong, to try to persuade people to change their beliefs.

You Invited Me In...

However bizarre this philosophy may sound to a Christian, it has a powerful impact on the lives of young adults today. In my two examples, what the young woman and the young man believed affected their behavior. Because of the influence of postmodern philosophy, 80% of young adults don't believe in or care about God. Which means when they die their eternal destinies will be hell. And, millions of young women have been convinced that they have the right to do whatever they please with their bodies, and that the babies they conceive are no more than unwanted tissue to be disposed of any way they choose. The very real result of that belief system has been almost 60 million aborted babies.

This is why, as Pentecostal, Bible-believing, Christians, we have to make sure that our theology is clear and Christ-centered. This is also why Yvonne and I believe it is vital for Pentecostal hospitality house military ministries to be established throughout our country that are intentionally, and strategically, focused on Jesus Christ.

We have to know what we believe and why we believe it. And, we have to be able to articulate it clearly to those who do not believe. Our words are important! And our philosophy of life matters! In Colossians 2:8 the Bible says,

> *See to it that no one takes you captive through hollow and deceptive philosophy, which depends on human tradition and the elemental spiritual forces of this world rather than on Christ.*

We cannot allow postmodern philosophy to determine our beliefs, and whether or not we communicate the Gospel of Jesus Christ to young military men and women. But we must also realize that by sharing the Christ-centered message of the Bible with them—by striving to help them believe that the Christ of that message is *really real*, we are going against the prevailing postmodern culture of our time. It will invite opposition. But it must be done, because the eternal destinies of these young men and women hang in the balance!

If our message is not clear, if it is not Christ-centered, and if young people do not understand it, Satan will come along and snatch away what they have heard. And yes, we believe that Satan is real and really does that! In Matthew 13:19 Jesus said:

When anyone hears the message about the kingdom and does not understand it, the evil one comes and snatches away what was sown in their heart.

And in Luke 8:12-13 Jesus explained why the evil one, or Satan, does this:

...the devil comes and takes away the word from their hearts, so that they may not believe and be saved.

It is the devil's purpose to oppose the proclamation of the gospel message, and to keep people from believing in Jesus Christ and being saved. So I will say it again: our message to young military men and women must be Christ-centered, and the words we use to share that message must be clear, concise, and unequivocal, if they are going to understand it and accept that most important of all messages.

But there is still another aspect of postmodern philosophy that impacts our young people today. That aspect says there is no unifying center around which all truth about reality revolves to form a unifying whole. Postmodern philosophers claim there is no single authority that establishes a common standard for defining all of reality; a standard by which all truth is measured. There are only differing opinions. And every opinion is equally valid, even if they are contradictory. And since there is no one to say which truth is right, then *every* truth is right.

That concept directly contradicts Colossians 1:16-17. Those verses (speaking about Jesus Christ) say,

> *For in him all things were created: things in heaven and on earth, visible and invisible, whether thrones or powers or rulers or authorities; all things have been created through him and for him. He is before all things, and in him all things hold together.*

According to this passage, Jesus Christ is real, and He is the Center of the universe. All things were created by Him and for Him, and all things are held together by Him.

Jesus said we would know the truth, and that the truth would set us free.[41] Many people ask the question: "What is truth?" Jesus answered that question when He said, "I am the way and the truth and the life."[42]

Because the effects of postmodern philosophy are so pervasive in our culture, we have to be intentional as Christians, and intense, in our focus on the Person and work of Jesus Christ as the Center of the Christian life and message. We must declare Him to be the Center of the universe, for He is the Center of all reality. And we must believe and declare that He is the single Authority Who establishes the common standard for defining all of reality. His Word is our all-sufficient rule of both faith and practice.

In this philosophical environment, when young adults say they believe in God, there is no easy way to know what "God" they are acknowledging, or what kind of spirituality they are practicing. When a young person says he or she believes in God, or that he or she has accepted God as Savior, which God are they talking about? Are they saying they believe in Jesus Christ? Or are they saying they believe in Allah, Buddha, Krishna, Vishnu,

---

[41] John 8:32.
[42] John 14:6.

or Jehovah? Is it possible they may be saying they believe in some combination of them all?

With the rapid advance of technology and instant access to the Internet, young adults today have access to an unimaginable amount of information about every religion in the world right on the cell phones they carry in their pockets! Many of these young people are able to pick and choose what they believe from all sorts of global religions and belief systems. They can reject what they don't like from each religious system, and merge what they do like from each one into their own personal "collage" of faith and practice.

So when a young person says I believe God is my Savior, he or she may be equating that with Jesus Christ alone. But that is far from certain. As a result, we have to choose our words carefully. We must articulate our meaning precisely so that the young people we talk to will hear and understand a clear, Christ-centered message.

If we do not focus on Jesus Christ, and share a clear gospel message with young military men and women, we are simply a nice old couple that plays games with and feeds these young people. That is alright, in and of itself, but it has no eternal consequences. What Yvonne and I do is meant to change and shape the eternal destinies of these young men and women. And the only way that can be done is by introducing them to Jesus Christ and helping them develop a personal relationship with Him.

The Christ-Centered Message

In our ministry, Yvonne and I never assume a serviceman or woman who comes into our home and participates in our activities is a Christian, even if they say they were raised in a Christian home and attended a Christian church. The focus of our Saturday night activities is on food, fun, and fellowship. However, when a new serviceman or woman joins our activities, a portion of the evening is dedicated to sharing personal testimonies, life stories, and the gospel message.

Most of the time we use the "Have You Heard of the Four Spiritual Laws?" pamphlet to present the gospel as simply and clearly as possible. We go around the room with everyone taking turns reading a couple of pages of the pamphlet. The tract ends with a suggested prayer for the reader to pray to invite Jesus Christ into their lives. We provide a time of silence at that point for anyone who wants to invite Jesus into their hearts to do so.

But beyond just reading through the pamphlet, I also highlight, expand, and explain certain aspects and truths. For example, I emphasize that God loves them and offers them eternal life through faith in Jesus Christ, "For God so loved the world that he gave his one and only Son, that whoever believes in him shall not perish but have eternal life."[43]

I also explain that it is our individual sins that separate us from God. I highlight that the Bible says, "For all have sinned and fall short of the glory of God…"[44] and that, "…the wages of sin is death, but the gift of God is eternal life in Christ Jesus our Lord."[45]

Because God is just, and *everyone* has sinned, everyone is under the same condemnation: eternal separation from God, and punishment in the fires of hell. This is not because God wants to send people to hell, but because His justice and holiness demand that sin be punished. So everyone on the planet is under the same condemnation.

However, besides being just, God is also a God of love. Out of His love, He has provided a way for people to be forgiven for their sins. As it says in 1 John 1:9, *"If we confess our sins, he is faithful and just and will forgive us our sins and purify us from all unrighteousness."* God the Father sent His Son Jesus Christ

---

[43] John 3:16.
[44] Romans 3:23.
[45] Romans 6:23.

You Shared Jesus with Me

to pay the penalty for our sins. And, just as the scripture in Romans 6:23 says, the wages of sin is death, so it also says the gift of God is eternal life. That life comes through faith in Jesus Christ.

I explain to them that in order to become a child of God and have our sins forgiven we must individually receive Jesus Christ as our Savior. We are not children of God because we are born as human beings. John 1:12 says, *"Yet to all who did receive him, to those who believed in his name, he gave the right to become children of God..."*

It isn't through a particular religion or church, doing good deeds, or simply being a human being that makes us children of God. It is through receiving Jesus Christ that we become God's children.

I go on to share that, according to John 3:3, we must all be "born again" to enter into the kingdom of God. Jesus says, *"...Very truly I tell you, no one can see the kingdom of God unless they are born again."* Jesus is saying that a person had to be born once, physically, in order to become a human being. In order to get into the kingdom of God, every single one of us must be born again (a *second* time), spiritually. The first birth is physical, the second birth is spiritual. That second birth is every bit as real as the first birth.

I also emphasize that if they invite Jesus into their lives, their lives will change according to 2 Corinthians 5:17, *"Therefore if any man be in Christ, he is a new creature: old things are passed away; behold, all things are become new."*[46] And I let them know that, according to Romans Chapter 10, verses 9 and 10, it is with the heart that a person believes, and with the mouth that confession is made and is saved.

This is the essence of our presentation of the gospel message. Scripture passages I highlight occasionally change, and we may

---

[46] KJV.

discuss certain parts in greater detail, depending on the questions that are asked or the comments that are made. But the message we share is always Christ-centered and focuses on the young man or woman's need to personally invite Jesus Christ into their lives and confess Him as Lord in order to be saved.

A Few of Our Stories

Let me share a few stories of our experiences with sharing the gospel message, beginning with one Christmas Eve when we received a telephone call from a young sailor on one of the ships home-ported at the Norfolk Naval Station. He was referred to us by his ship's chaplain, and asked about our ministry activities. All of the other servicemen in our ministry had gone home on Christmas leave, so we had not planned any group activities. Yvonne and I were going to eat dinner and then attend a Christmas Eve candlelight service at a local church. But we didn't want to turn him away, so we invited him to join us for dinner and to attend the church service with us if he wanted to. He accepted our invitation, and we all had a nice evening together.

As I drove him back to his ship, the young man lamented that the one thing he really wanted was a Spanish Bible. I just happened to have two in my library, so I turned the car around, went back to the house, and gave him one. We sat in the parking lot in front of his ship until 1:30 in the morning, talking about Jesus Christ and the plan of salvation. Before getting out of the car, he prayed and invited Jesus into his life.

On another Saturday evening a young sailor who had been coming to the house for a while, was the only person who came over that night. We ate, played a board game, and had a pleasant evening together. Right after the game, we got involved in a discussion about world problems and how they could be solved. I have to admit, it was unusual to go from playing a board game to such a serious conversation.

But for me, the answer to even the most enormous problems of the world come down to dealing with the issue of sin. And that can only be done on an individual basis, by individuals turning away from sin and receiving Jesus Christ as their Savior. So I explained that to him. He asked how a person does that.

I asked him if he had ever heard of the four spiritual laws? He said he had not. So I shared them with him. When we came to the suggested prayer and the opportunity to invite Jesus into his heart, he stopped me and asked a question I will never forget.

He had been raised in the church, but had drifted away. He asked, "Do you think God will take me back?"

I was really shocked by the question, but without hesitating for a moment, I said, "YES! Absolutely! In a heartbeat! God loves you!" After which he smiled, bowed his head and invited Jesus to come into his heart.

Sometimes, during our Saturday evening or Sunday afternoon activities, we watch Christian themed DVDs such as The Climb; Time Changer; The Cross and the Switchblade; Facing the Giants, or Fireproof. Or, we watch Bible DVDs like The Gospel of Matthew, The Gospel of John, or Acts. Each of these DVDs portray a clear presentation of the gospel message in dramatic ways.

One particular Sunday afternoon, we watched and discussed the Christian video called "The Omega Code 2." It's a very intense and dramatic presentation about the end-time events in the Bible. One young sailor and his wife, who were usually the first to leave when our activities were over, stayed behind that afternoon. After some hesitation, the sailor's wife asked how a person could accept Jesus Christ as their Savior, because she wanted to be ready when the end times occurred. We explained how she could invite Jesus into her life, and asked her if she wanted to do that. She said yes, bowed her head, and invited Him into her heart.

A significant part of every Saturday evening and Sunday afternoon occurs at the end of the day's activities. We encourage everyone to share prayer needs and participate in the prayer time for those needs. If anyone is sick, we anoint them with oil in the Name of the Lord Jesus Christ and lay hands on the sick person, as instructed in James, Chapter 5, and pray for their healing.

We also gather around and lay hands on a soldier or sailor who is about to be transferred to another duty station, and pray for their safety in travel and a good adjustment to their new command.

During one of our regular prayer times one of our young sailors shared a prayer request for a friend he knew through an online gaming environment. This friend was only 28 years old, but was dying with stage-four cancer. He had been receiving chemotherapy treatments, but had only been given three to six months to live by his doctors.

We began praying for him regularly. And a few months later, our sailor shared the news that the young man was getting better. His cancer was in remission. When our sailor went home on Christmas leave, he went to see his recovering friend. When he came back, he told us the young man no longer had cancer, and that his hair was even growing back. What an awesome example of God's ability and willingness to answer prayer, and of His healing power!

Conclusion

These are just a few of the stories of the servicemen and women and their families that have been through our home, heard the gospel message, and responded to that message. There have been 30 men and women who have either invited Jesus Christ into their lives for the first time or recommitted their lives to him in our home.

Hopefully, from this explanation and the stories we've shared, you can see how important providing a safe, comfortable, home and family environment is for young servicemen and women. And, how having regularly-scheduled, enjoyable social activities in that environment prepares the way for establishing close personal relationships with them.

We also hope you can see how these elements, combined with a clear Christ-centered articulation of the gospel message, all work together to increase their willingness to listen to the presentation of the gospel, and invite Jesus Christ into their lives.

However, this is still not the end of the story. In the next three chapters we'll discuss what we do in our ministry *after* a young man or woman invites Christ into their lives.

8

YOU SHARED THE CHRISTIAN LIFE WITH ME

Yvonne and I work with young military men and women to share the gospel with them and introduce them to Jesus Christ. But, our ministry efforts don't end there. We want to help them understand what their new relationship with Christ means and how to develop their walk with Him.

One soldier said her relationship with Jesus Christ was just beginning when she started attending our activities and summarized her experience with us like this:

"During the time that I was there, I was just learning about what being a Christian was. Honestly, I probably only came because it was a chance to hang out with my friends and eat a good meal in a relaxed atmosphere. I wouldn't say that [your ministry]¹ necessarily changed anything for me, but it was more of something that I observed and it was an example for me to see Christians come together and spend time together, talk about the Lord, and pray together. The whole praying thing with prayer requests was really strange to me, because I've

never seen anyone do that before, and even praying for the small things in life. I guess I hadn't realized that the Lord was so close to us, and that he hears us all the time when we call out to him. Now, two years later, I can look back to the time spent at [your ministry] and it all makes a whole lot more sense. I think that everything we did there was awesome..."

Introducing a soldier or a sailor to Jesus Christ is just the beginning. Teaching them about the Christian life and modeling that life in front of them is also part of our work. Yvonne and I try to help servicemen and women make the connection between their new intellectual knowledge of Jesus Christ and the Bible, and their actual behavior.

One of the first ways we try to help them make that connection is in the physical act of water baptism by immersion after they decide to follow Christ. At the conclusion of our activities one Sunday afternoon, we were all standing by the front door saying goodbye. I was talking to one of the sailors about being water baptized. A female marine who was listening to our conversation said she had invited Jesus into her heart at our Christmas party four months earlier. She wondered if I thought she should be water baptized, too. After talking with her for a few minutes, I said yes, she should be baptized, too.

Since she was leaving for a new assignment soon, we scheduled a water baptism service on the beach on Little Creek Naval Amphibious Base for Easter Sunday afternoon. Both the sailor and the marine were baptized, with the rest of our group standing on the beach watching.

Much of what happens in our home involves watching, listening, considering, and finally deciding. The word "mentoring" is often used to describe this type of modeling and instruction. Because the schedules of servicemen and women are so transient, the opportunity to engage in extensive, structured

You Shared the Christian Life with Me

instruction does not present itself very often. So as we get together for our weekly activities, most of what we do is informal and spontaneous. We watch for, and take advantage of frequent "teachable moments" that present themselves.

Discipleship

In 1994, Yvonne and I attended the North American Conference for Itinerant Evangelists in Louisville, Kentucky, hosted by the Billy Graham Evangelistic Association. The conference brought together 3,000 itinerant evangelists from around the world, to encourage and equip them for the task of reaching men and women with the gospel of Jesus Christ. Transcripts of the conference speakers' presentations were compiled in a book entitled *Equipping for Evangelism*.

In the conference keynote address, Billy Graham said, "We must get back to the simplicity of the gospel because so many want Christ but don't know how to find Him. They have never heard it in simple, everyday language which they can understand."[47]

A case in point is a good friend of mine who was raised in an evangelical, Bible-believing church. After a lengthy conversation one summer, I asked him if he had ever asked Jesus Christ to come into his life. He said he had not. When I asked him why, he simply said he didn't know how. He said no one had ever explained *how* he could receive Jesus as his Savior. I explained it to him, and we prayed together. My friend invited Jesus into his heart and life.

As important as it is to present a simple message that is understandable, it is equally important to be clear concerning exactly what that "message" is, and how it should impact a

---

[47] Billy Graham, "The evangelist in a changing world: it's a new day," *NACIE 94 Equipping For Evangelism: North American Conference for Itinerant Evangelists*, ed. Charles Ward, (Minneapolis: World Wide Publications), 1996, p. 21.

person's life in the long run. At the NACIE '94 conference, Lewis Drummond said, "To put it in simple summary form, we call people to repentance and faith. Away with the superficiality of mere decision making...." Explaining the meaning of the word repentance, he said it means, "....to change one's mind concerning God, Christ, and the gospel. It means to change one's emotions, that is, instead of feeling repulsed, one feels drawn to the Lord Jesus Christ, turns to the Lord, and runs to the cross...."[48]

Many Christian authors have criticized overt evangelistic methods, either crusade or personal, which challenge an audience or an individual to "make a decision" for Jesus Christ. Their criticism is that there is much more involved with becoming a Christian than simply "making a decision." And while I agree with that statement, it is at the point of decision making, of inviting Jesus into one's life and asking Him for forgiveness and turning from a life of sin or indifference to Him, that the new life begins. It is at that point in time that a person is "born again." A point in a person's life every bit as real as the moment of their physical birth.

Therefore, Yvonne and I regularly give the young men and women who come into our home the opportunity to make that decision for Jesus Christ. And then we go on to help them understand what that decision means for the rest their lives.

In his book, *Psychology for Successful Evangelism*, James Jauncey described the message the Apostle Paul preached as the announcement of the death, burial, and resurrection of Christ. He said this was never intended to be "a mere matter of academic interest" but that "the hearer was being challenged by it to believe and commit his life to Christ in faith. Jauncey said the hearer's response would, "soon evaporate unless it was

---

[48] Lewis Drummond, 1996. "What is the message?" In *NACIE 94 Equipping For Evangelism: North American Conference for Itinerant Evangelists*, ed. Charles Ward, 41. (Minneapolis: World Wide Publications). 1996.

conserved," and went on to say that this conservation was done through "public confession" and "identification with the Christian fellowship."[49]

He gave a unique description of the psychological aspect of the conversion process when he said, "Committal to Christ involves committal to His way of living...the convert must be taught this way....But, like the preaching, this teaching is not academic. It presupposes a continual positive response so that the life is rebuilt on that foundation."[50]

He goes on to say, "Evangelism is intended to be much more than persuading people to make decisions, and it covers much more than conversion. Jesus has in mind a total change in being, a complete reorientation, a permanent 'set' of the personality to His philosophy of living."[51] Explaining why many new converts turn away from the decision they make, Jauncey says, "To make a decision for Christ isn't too hard. A person can be made to see that this is in the best interest of the self, and the will may OK it. But unless some work has already been done on the unconscious, the whole 'set' of the personality will be pulling in the opposite direction, creating an almost insufferable burden."[52]

He summarizes this psychological evangelism-conversion process saying:

> Thus, the study of the unconscious puts evangelism in its true perspective as a long process that affects man's deepest being. Unless adequate work has already been done on the unconscious, any hit-or-miss, one-shot attempts to bring about a decision will be meaningless. If, however, the preparation has been adequate, a single challenge may very well be all that is required to trigger

---

[49] James Jauncey, *Psychology for Successful Evangelism*. 17. (Chicago: Moody Press). 1972.
[50] Ibid.
[51] Jauncey, 18.
[52] Jauncey, 20.

off the spiritual revolution. But even then it must not be left there. The new personality orientation must be reinforced and made permanent by subsequent buildup of spiritual factors. Then the whole man will belong to God, and his evangelization will be complete.[53]

So, presenting a clear and understandable message is the key to achieving success in the evangelism process, which involves far more than merely getting an individual to "make a decision." It is the transformation of the person's entire being from a state of rebellion against, or simply indifference toward, Jesus Christ to one of total commitment to and intimate personal relationship with Him as Savior and Lord.

Jauncey describes the human need to "belong" in the context of evangelism:

> We have to feel important and needed, not only to people at large, but to a group or groups, even though the group may comprise only two people. This can never be superficial if we are going to be satisfied. We must feel that we are absolutely necessary to the welfare and happiness of others besides ourselves. We must be convinced that they care so much about us that they are as anxious about us as they are about themselves.[54]

This need is even more pronounced when combined with the loneliness and home sickness often experienced by young military men and women. Dr. Lawrence J. Crabb, Jr. wrote of the need for relationship in his book, *Understanding People: Deep Longings for Relationship* when he said, "We long to be in relationship with someone who is strong enough to be constant, someone whose love is untainted by even a trace of

---

[53] Jauncey, 22.
[54] Jauncey, 56.

manipulative self-interest, someone who really wants us."[55] It's because of this intense need to belong that reaching out to lonely, separated young military men and women in a home and family environment is so important. Jauncey gave an example of relational outreach similar to what Yvonne and I do saying,

> A member couple invites another couple with whom they are acquainted to a nonreligious gathering of the class: a party or a picnic or a bowling evening. The new couple is made particularly welcome and quickly gets to like the group. In no time at all, this inner drive to belong welds them into spiritual integration with the group. They find they have a built-in inclination to accept the group's religious goals before they even know about them. It becomes an easy step to graduate from the social functions to the religious activities. Then when the time is ripe they readily take the final step of personal committal to Christ.[56]

Many people today feel that clergy are unapproachable. Rebecca Pippert, in her book, *Out of the Salt Shaker*, commented, "The people of Jesus' day thought holy men were unapproachable. But Jesus' work was in the marketplace. He made people feel welcome, and that they had a place."[57] It's been our experience that many young servicemen and women who come to us for help or spiritual guidance, apologize for "interrupting" us, or for "bothering" us. We frequently have to reassure them that they are the reason our ministry exists and that they are not a bother nor an interruption.

---

[55] Lawrence J. Crabb, *Understanding People: Deep Longings for Relationship*. 112. (Grand Rapids: Zondervan Publishing House). 1987.
[56] Jauncey, 59-60.
[57] Pippert, Rebecca M. *Out of the Saltshaker & Into the World*. 36. (Downers Grove: InterVarsity Press). 1979.

Pippert goes on to observe in the life of Christ that, "Jesus established intimacy with people quickly....because he understood people and wanted to establish rapport."[58] She noted, "In Jesus, then, we have our model for how to relate to the world, and it is a model of openness and identification."[59] She concluded, "We must learn then to relate transparently and genuinely to others because that's God's style of relating to us....we must open our lives enough to let people see that we too laugh and hurt and cry."[60]

Robert Coleman, writing in, *The Master Plan of Evangelism*, arrived at a similar conclusion, saying, "...those persons to whom we open our lives will come to see our many shortcomings. But let them also see a readiness to confess our sins when we understand the error of our way. Let them hear us apologize to those we have wronged. Our weaknesses need not impair discipleship when shining through them is a transparent sincerity to follow Christ."[61]

Intimate association and fellowship is a key to in-depth relational evangelism. Communicating the gospel of Jesus Christ is more than "preaching." It is sharing life. Jesus' disciples were known even by their critics as men who "had been with" Jesus. Coleman said Jesus' disciples gained knowledge by their association with Him long before they were given explanations of truths.[62] Applying this principle to modern-day believers, Coleman said we must "show" people what we mean rather than merely telling them what we mean.[63]

In summarizing Jesus' relationship with His disciples, Coleman said, "He ate with them, slept with them, and talked

---

[58] Pippert, 36.
[59] Pippert, 34.
[60] Ibid.
[61] Coleman, Robert E. *The Master Plan of Evangelism*. 77. (Grand Rapids: Fleming H. Revell). 1993.
[62] Coleman, 42.
[63] Coleman, 76.

You Shared the Christian Life with Me

with them for the most part His entire active ministry. They walked together along the lonely roads; they visited together in the crowded cities; they sailed and fished together on the Sea of Galilee; they prayed together in the deserts and in the mountains; and they worshipped together in the synagogues and in the Temple."[64] Jesus shared his life with His disciples and lived out the gospel message in front of them. He showed them how to evangelize the lost as they lived their lives.

This is the kind of transparency Yvonne and I strive for in our relationships with the servicemen and women who come into our home. As we eat together, play board games, go on day trips, watch television, and even worship and pray together, we try to model what it means to be Christ-like. Hopefully, they will see the love of Jesus in us and be more open to listen to our presentation of the gospel message and be drawn to Him.

Steve Sjogren wrote, *Conspiracy of Kindness*, and talks about what he calls "servant evangelism." This, he says, is the kind of ministry in which believers serve others, free of charge, to show them the love of Christ. About his outreach efforts, he says, "Our service to the community is always free. Many people offer to donate to our 'cause,' but we always refuse any repayment. To receive money for what we do would lessen the impact of our services. Free service offers a picture of the grace of God, a priceless gift which can never be repaid."[65] These are the very reasons, in all of the things Yvonne and I do in our ministry, we never "charge" the servicemen and women who participate with us for the food they receive, or the entrance fees to our special events activities.

Sjogren goes on to say, "Even though people aren't conscious of what's happening, they are welcoming us and the God we represent into the fortress of their hearts. Deeds of love

---

[64] Coleman, 45.
[65] Steve Sjogren, *Conspiracy of Kindness,* (Ann Arbor: Servant Publications), 1993, p. 19.

aren't enough on their own to bring someone to Christ, but they do create 'phone wires' for transmitting the spoken message."[66] He made the very significant observation that, "If we don't follow our actions with words, they will only know that we are nice people, not that God loves them."[67] Many of the men and women involved in our ministry have told us they were more willing to listen to our presentation of the gospel message because of the environment we provided and the relationships that they formed with us.

As in any family, we hope our "children" will make good choices when they leave home and move out on their own. While they are stationed here we hope that our example, our love, and the nurture we provide, will enable them to grow in their Christian life to the point where, when they get transferred to other duty stations, they will be able to continue living for the Lord.

Methods and Tools

We use a wide variety of tools in our discipleship of the servicemen and women who become part of our family. We've already mentioned that we watch DVDs such as The Climb, Time Changer, Facing the Giants, Courageous, Fireproof, and many others, that dramatically present nuggets of truth about how to live the Christian life. We also watch Bible videos to illustrate the scriptures in an interesting and dramatic way. And, we regularly watch video series designed to present a biblical world view such as the one created by Focus on the Family

---

[66] Sjogren, 23.
[67] Ibid.

You Shared the Christian Life with Me

called *The Truth Project*[68]; and another called *Origins: How the World Came to Be* by Films for Christ.[69]

Modern technology and social media also play a large part in our ability to communicate with the young men and women involved in our ministry. When we first began this ministry phone calls and emails were the primary way we communicated with them. Now we communicate primarily through texting on our cell phones and on Facebook. Yvonne and I often receive text messages asking questions about the Bible or for personal advice and guidance.

Doctoral Research

As part of the research for my doctorate, I wanted to know how the servicemen and women who had been involved in our ministry felt about the impact we had on their lives. In the survey I mentioned previously, the forty-six people who completed the survey provided some very pleasing and encouraging feedback. Let me share some of that with you.

A significant emphasis in the discipleship aspect of our ministry is helping servicemen and women make the connection between their *intellectual* knowledge of the Bible and their *behavior*. Thirty-five of the 46 who responded said they learned that this connection existed while they were involved with us. Forty-one said their understanding of at least some portion of the Bible improved as a result of participating in our ministry. It was really encouraging when 31 people said they decided to be more obedient to Jesus Christ and His teachings as a result of their involvement with us. Thirty-four said they decided to live more committed Christian lives; and 39 said their relationship with

---

[68] Dr. Del Tackett, *The Truth Project,* (Colorado Springs, CO: Focus on the Family, 2011).
[69] Dr. A.E. Wilder-Smith, *Origins: How the World Came to Be*, (Marysville, WA: Films for Christ, 1983).

You Invited Me In...

Jesus Christ was either closer or *much* closer as a result of the time they spent with us.

So, for Yvonne and me, opening our home to servicemen and women, providing a safe and comfortable home and family environment for them, eating together, and playing games together, prepares the way for the establishment of close personal relationships. Providing free, enjoyable, and regularly scheduled social activities helps develop those relationships, and increases a willingness in them to listen to the gospel message. Articulating that message clearly, with a specific focus on Jesus Christ, increases a soldier, sailor, or marine's understanding of the gospel and helps them accept Jesus Christ as their Savior, grow in their relationship with Him, and choose to live a more committed Christian life.

But once again, this is still not the end of the process. A significant part of our discipleship emphasis is the baptism with the Holy Spirit. That baptism is a spiritual experience subsequent to salvation for the divine empowerment of a person to be a witness for Jesus Christ. In the next two chapters, I'll focus on these aspects of our discipleship of servicemen and women.

9

YOU SHARED THE HOLY SPIRIT WITH ME

A young marine who was raised in a Pentecostal home, but who had never been baptized with the Holy Spirit, began attending our weekend activities. One Sunday afternoon when we were talking about Spirit baptism, he said he always wanted to be baptized with the Holy Spirit. He said he had often prayed to be Spirit-baptized while growing up, but never was. So we gathered around him, anointed him with oil, laid hands on him, and prayed that Jesus would baptize him with the Holy Spirit. As far as we could tell nothing happen, and we went back to talking and fellowshipping and concluded our afternoon activity.

The young man went home for two weeks on Christmas leave. When his leave period ended, Yvonne and I picked him up at the airport to give him a ride back to his base.

As we loaded his luggage into the trunk of our car he said, "Guess what happened to me while I was at home?"

I smiled and said, "I don't know, what happened?"

With a big grin he said, "I was baptized with the Holy Spirit and spoke in tongues!"

You Invited Me In...

He said, "I was so excited about it that I could hardly wait to get back to tell you!" The Lord answered our prayer!

What is the Baptism with the Holy Spirit?

The baptism with the Holy Spirit, according to Acts 1:8, is a spiritual experience subsequent to salvation, through which a person receives divine power to be a witness for Jesus Christ. This experience originated with the disciples 50 days after Jesus' resurrection, and is recorded by Luke in Acts 2:1-4. The day is commonly referred to as the Day of Pentecost in the Christian Church, and is where the term *Pentecostal* comes from.

In this chapter, I want to talk about the baptism with the Holy Spirit in detail from a biblical perspective. And I want to share how being baptized with the Holy Spirit applies to our ministry with the young military men and women who come into our home.

John the Baptist's Prophecy

Being baptized with the Holy Spirit begins with an understanding of John the Baptist's prophecy that Jesus Christ would baptize people with the Holy Spirit. His prophecy is included in all four of the Gospels: Matthew, Mark, Luke and John. Matthew records John's prophecy this way:

> *I baptize you with water for repentance. But after me comes one who is more powerful than I, whose sandals I am not worthy to carry. He will baptize you with the Holy Spirit and fire. His winnowing fork is in his hand, and he will clear his threshing floor, gathering his wheat into the barn and burning up the chaff with unquenchable fire.*[70]

---

[70] Matthew 3:11-12. See also Mark 1:8, Luke 3:16, and John 1:33.

You Shared the Holy Spirit with Me

The prophecy refers to two separate baptisms on two separate groups of people. The first is the baptism with the Holy Spirit, and the second is a baptism with fire. The first applies to the power to preach the salvation message, the second applies to the judgment of people who reject that message. The group of people baptized with the Holy Spirit are Christian believers, while the group baptized with fire are non-believers. In both instances Jesus Christ is doing the baptizing.

In Matthew 3, verse 12, John the Baptist mentions Jesus holding a winnowing fork in His hand to clear His threshing floor. John is referring to the same two events. The gathering of the wheat into the barn is a reference to those who are saved and gathered into Jesus' Kingdom. The burning up of the chaff refers to the final judgment of unbelievers and their eternal destiny in hell.

Preaching the Message of Salvation

Each of the gospel writers included Jesus' post-resurrection appearance to His disciples. Before His ascension, He gave them a mandate, which was to go and make disciples of all nations. Matthew recorded the mandate this way:

> *Therefore go and make disciples of all nations, baptizing them in the name of the Father and of the Son and of the Holy Spirit, and teaching them to obey everything I have commanded you.*[71]

Matthew sets these elements between two statements Jesus made in which He said, all authority in heaven and on earth was given to Him; *and* that He would be with the disciples to the very end of the age.

---

[71] Matthew 28:19-20.

Jesus' disciples were to carry on their evangelistic work on the authority Jesus had received from God the Father, and which He was delegating to them. And, as they exercised their delegated authority and performed their evangelistic work, Jesus would be with them.

Mark recorded Jesus' commission to His disciples as one in which their work would be accompanied by divine signs and wonders. Those signs and wonders would be accomplished by the Lord *through* the disciples, in confirmation of the salvation message they preached.

> *He said to them, "Go into all the world and preach the gospel to all creation. Whoever believes and is baptized will be saved, but whoever does not believe will be condemned. And these signs will accompany those who believe: In my name they will drive out demons; they will speak in new tongues; they will pick up snakes with their hands; and when they drink deadly poison, it will not hurt them at all; they will place their hands on sick people, and they will get well." After the Lord Jesus had spoken to them, he was taken up into heaven and he sat at the right hand of God. Then the disciples went out and preached everywhere, and the Lord worked with them and confirmed his word by the signs that accompanied it.*[72]

The writer of Hebrews acknowledged these signs and wonders and the gifts of the Spirit when he said:

> *This salvation, which was first announced by the Lord, was confirmed to us by those who heard him. God also testified to it by signs, wonders and various*

---

[72] Mark 16:15-20.

miracles, and by gifts of the Holy Spirit distributed according to his will.[73]

The testimony of these Scriptures is that the message of the gospel of Jesus Christ is to be proclaimed by Jesus' followers in the power of the Holy Spirit and would be confirmed with supernatural signs and wonders.

The Purpose of the Baptism with the Holy Spirit

In the Gospel of John, Jesus told His disciples,

As my Father hath sent me, so send I you.[74]

He also said,

Very truly I tell you, whoever believes in me will do the works I have been doing, and they will do even greater things than these, because I am going to the Father.[75]

In light of Jesus' statement, the question arises, "What were the works of Jesus?"

The answer is that He proclaimed the message of salvation—the forgiveness of sins and eternal life through faith in Him—and confirmed that message with accompanying miraculous signs and wonders. So, Jesus was saying that as His disciples preached the Word to unbelievers, in the power of the Holy Spirit, Jesus would work with them to confirm the Word they preached with the same kinds of signs and wonders He had performed. But this was not something they would be able to do in their own human ability.

---

[73] Hebrews 2:3-4.
[74] John 20:21, KJV.
[75] John 14:12.

You Invited Me In...

Jesus knew that after His ascension, His disciples would need supernatural empowerment to fulfill His mandate to make disciples of all nations. Luke recorded Jesus' prophecy about that future impartation of power in Luke 24:46-49, saying:

This is what is written: The Christ will suffer and rise from the dead on the third day, and repentance and forgiveness of sins will be preached in His name to all nations, beginning at Jerusalem. You are witnesses of these things. I am going to send you what my Father has promised; but stay in the city until you have been clothed with power from on high.[76]

The disciples were to wait in the city until they received supernatural power before they went out to evangelize. But, the question that comes to mind is, "How would the disciples know when they had received that supernatural power?"

The answer is found in the Book of Acts Chapter 1:4-6. In this passage Luke connects Jesus' prophecy of the disciples' receiving the "promise of the Father" with John the Baptist's prophecy that Jesus would baptize people with the Holy Spirit:

To whom also he shewed himself alive after his passion by many infallible proofs, being seen of them forty days, and speaking of the things pertaining to the kingdom of God: And, being assembled together with them, commanded them that they should not depart from Jerusalem, but wait for the promise of the Father, which, saith he, ye have heard of me. For John truly baptized with water; but ye shall be baptized with the Holy Ghost not many days hence.[77]

---

[76] Luke 24:46-49, KJV.
[77] Acts 1:4-6, KJV.

You Shared the Holy Spirit with Me

Then in Acts 1:8, Luke connected Jesus' prophecy and John the Baptist's prophecy with the impartation of divine power to be Jesus' witnesses throughout the world.

> *But ye shall receive power, after that the Holy Ghost is come upon you: and ye shall be witnesses unto me both in Jerusalem, and in all Judaea, and in Samaria, and unto the uttermost part of the earth.*[78]

It's important to understand the connections between these prophecies in order to understand their fulfillment, and to answer the question, "How did the disciples know when they had received supernatural power?" It is also important to understand that in Acts 1:8 Jesus explained that the *purpose* of the baptism with the Holy Spirit was to receive *power* to be His witnesses throughout the world.

The Fulfillment of the Prophecies

The fulfillment of the prophecies about Spirit-baptism occurred on the Day of Pentecost and was recorded by Luke in Acts 2:1-4:

> *When the day of Pentecost came, they were all together in one place. Suddenly a sound like the blowing of a violent wind came from heaven and filled the whole house where they were sitting. They saw what seemed to be tongues of fire that separated and came to rest on each of them. All of them were filled with the Holy Spirit and began to speak in other tongues as the Spirit enabled them.*[79]

---

[78] Acts 1:8, KJV.
[79] Acts 2:1-4.

You Invited Me In...

The disciples were all gathered together in one place, in an upper room. Several physical manifestations occurred, including the sound of a rushing wind, visible tongues of fire resting on the disciples' heads, and each of the disciples audibly speaking in "other tongues," languages that were not their own. The Holy Spirit had come upon them.

This experience confirmed to the disciples that they had received the "promise of the Father" that Jesus had prophesied in Luke 24, and that they had received "power" to be Jesus' witnesses. Peter explained it to the crowd in Jerusalem this way,

> *God has raised this Jesus to life, and we are all witnesses of it. Exalted to the right hand of God, he has received from the Father the promised Holy Spirit and has poured out what you now see and hear.*[80]

Was this experience just for that first group of disciples in that upper room? Or would it be for other believers as well?

For the answer to these questions we have to continue looking at Peter's explanation where he said,

> *The promise is for you and your children and for all who are far off—for all whom the Lord our God will call.*[81]

Peter viewed this promise as a generational promise. The way he worded his answer begins with the generation he was talking to – *you*. It continued with the next generation – *your children*. And was to go on to every succeeding generation – *all who are far off*.

We've established that the disciples' experience *would* be repeated. When they are, would the signs be repeated as well? Would there be an identifiable *pattern*?

---

[80] Acts 2:32-33.
[81] Acts 2:39.

Luke mentions two other accounts of believers receiving the baptism with the Holy Spirit in the Book of Acts. The first is in the house of a Roman Centurion named Cornelius in Chapter 10:44-47. At the instruction of an angel, Cornelius called for Peter to come to his home. He then called his household together to listen to what Peter had to say. Luke's account says,

While Peter was still speaking these words, the Holy Spirit came on all who heard the message. The circumcised believers who had come with Peter were astonished that the gift of the Holy Spirit had been poured out even on Gentiles. For they heard them speaking in tongues and praising God. Then Peter said, "Surely no one can stand in the way of their being baptized with water. They have received the Holy Spirit just as we have."[82]

Peter's proclamation of the gospel was positively received by those of Cornelius' household who were gathered to listen. Immediately after they believed the message of salvation the Holy Spirit was poured out upon them; they were baptized with the Holy Spirit. Luke notes that Peter and those with him knew what had happened because they heard them speaking in tongues. The Spirit-baptism of Cornelius' household confirmed to the Jewish disciples that God had accepted the Gentiles as believers also.

The second account is the experience of the disciples from the Ephesian church who met with Paul in Chapter 19:1-7. Luke records Paul's meeting with them and their discussion about the Holy Spirit:

---

[82] Acts 10:44-47.

> *While Apollos was at Corinth, Paul took the road through the interior and arrived at Ephesus. There he found some disciples and asked them, 'Did you receive the Holy Spirit when you believed?' They answered, 'No, we have not even heard that there is a Holy Spirit.' So Paul asked, 'Then what baptism did you receive?' 'John's baptism,' they replied. Paul said, 'John's baptism was a baptism of repentance. He told the people to believe in the one coming after him, that is, in Jesus.' On hearing this, they were baptized in the name of the Lord Jesus. When Paul placed his hands on them, the Holy Spirit came on them, and they spoke in tongues and prophesied. There were about twelve men in all.*[83]

Following the disciples' baptism in water, Paul laid his hands on them, and the Holy Spirit came on them. Again, Luke records that the Ephesian believers spoke in tongues. Their experience illustrated the beginning of the spread of the gospel to the uttermost parts of the earth.

In each of these three accounts, the Day of Pentecost, Cornelius' household, and the Ephesian disciples, Luke records several phenomenon that occurred when believers were baptized with the Holy Spirit. These included a mighty wind, flames of fire, praising God, prophesying, and speaking in tongues. The one consistent and recurring phenomenon was *speaking in tongues*.

We believe from these accounts that it can be reasoned, for Luke, the normative initial evidence of receiving the baptism with the Holy Spirit is speaking in other tongues. It can also be reasoned that for those receiving the baptism with the Holy Spirit today, that the biblical *pattern* for the initial evidence of

---

[83] Acts 19:1-7.

You Shared the Holy Spirit with Me

Spirit-baptism is speaking in other tongues. Other phenomenon may occur, but all who are Spirit-baptized will speak in other tongues.

Boldness in the Face of Opposition

Fear and timidity in the face of opposition were issues that the disciples had to deal with in their preaching of the gospel, and rightly so. Having witnessed the brutal torture and execution of Jesus, and not wanting the same to happen to them, the disciples met behind locked doors on Easter Sunday morning for "fear of the Jews."[84]

Luke later records the disciples' newly acquired courage and boldness in the face of Jewish opposition after the Day of Pentecost in Acts Chapter 3 and 4. In these chapters Peter and John were used by the Lord to heal a crippled man. They were also preaching about faith in Jesus Christ, repentance and forgiveness in His Name. The Jewish religious authorities heard of their activities and came, seized them and put them in jail overnight.

They brought Peter and John in and questioned them about their activities. Peter responded to their inquiry by telling them about Jesus and concluding with this bold assertion:

Salvation is found in no one else, for there is no other name under heaven given to mankind by which we must be saved.[85]

The Jewish leaders were surprised at Peter's boldness! And in Acts 4:13 Luke records their reaction:

---

[84] John 20:19.
[85] Acts 4:12.

You Invited Me In...

> *When they saw the courage of Peter and John and realized that they were unschooled, ordinary men, they were astonished and they took note that these men had been with Jesus.*

After considering what they should do, the Jewish leaders called the disciples in again and gave them a command. They were ordered:

> *...not to speak or teach at all in the name of Jesus. But Peter and John replied, "Which is right in God's eyes: to listen to you, or to him? You be the judges! As for us, we cannot help speaking about what we have seen and heard."*[86]

This was a major change in the disciples' courage and boldness. Going from hiding for fear of the Jews on the first Easter Sunday morning, to being willing to confront them with the message of salvation, and refusing to keep silent about Jesus. The difference between these two attitudes was the disciples' baptism with the Holy Spirit on the Day of Pentecost.

Paul also addressed the problem of fear and timidity in preaching the gospel in the face of opposition, in his letter to Timothy, the young pastor of the church in Ephesus. In 2 Timothy 1:5-14, the Apostle acknowledged Timothy's "sincere faith."[87] But proceeds to admonish him that God has not given him a spirit of timidity, but a spirit of power, love, and self-discipline.[88] He then encouraged Timothy not to be "ashamed to testify about our Lord."[89]

---

[86] Acts 4:18-20.
[87] 2 Timothy 1:5.
[88] 2 Timothy 1:7.
[89] 2 Timothy 1:8.

You Shared the Holy Spirit with Me

Paul went on, using himself as an example of the kind of persecution and suffering that can accompany the preaching of the gospel. Yet he firmly declared that in the face of all he suffered, he was still "not ashamed."[90] He also lifted up Onesiphorus as an example of someone who was not ashamed to be associated with him in spite of his persecutions.

Paul encouraged Timothy to be strong in the grace that was in Jesus Christ. The Apostle was not only holding himself and Onesiphorus up as examples for the young pastor to emulate, he also reminded Timothy of Jesus Christ Himself and His sufferings. In 2 Timothy 2:15 the Apostle encouraged Timothy to present himself to God as one who was not ashamed, and who correctly handled the Word of Truth.[91] Paul's entire second epistle to Timothy was written to encourage the young pastor to be strong and faithful in the proclamation of the gospel message, even in the face of persecution.

While not clearly stated in the text, it is in light of this context that we believe 2 Timothy 1:6 is a reference to the Apostle's meeting with the Ephesian disciples in Acts 19:1-7. There, Paul laid his hands on the Ephesian disciples and they were baptized with the Holy Spirit. And again, while not specifically stated in the text, it is possible that Timothy was present at that meeting, and that he too had been baptized with the Holy Spirit through the laying on of the Apostle's hands.

Thus he would have received the divine impartation of power to be a witness for Jesus Christ which accompanies Spirit-baptism. So in our verse in 2 Timothy 1:6 the apostle was instructing Timothy to "fan into flame"[92] the gift he had received—the divine power of the Holy Spirit to be a witness for Jesus Christ.

---

[90] 2 Timothy 1:12.
[91] 2 Timothy 2:15.
[92] 2 Timothy 1:6.

Gateway to the Gifts of the Spirit

Spirit-baptism is also the initial experience through which a Christian is enabled to function in the biblical gifts of the Spirit. In addition to providing personal boldness to proclaim the gospel to unbelievers in one's sphere of influence, the Spirit-baptized believer is also enabled by the Holy Spirit to minister through divine power encounters.

Many Pentecostal believers are familiar with the three verbal gifts of the Spirit (speaking in tongues, the interpretation of tongues, and prophecy) because they have historically functioned during corporate worship services in Pentecostal churches. But, in 1 Corinthians 12:1-11, Paul lists nine gifts of the Holy Spirit. We believe it is through the use of all of these gifts, in the context of witnessing to non-believers about Jesus Christ, that great power to witness is manifested.

As Spirit-baptized believers share their faith in Jesus Christ with non-believing friends and acquaintances, and even strangers, the Holy Spirit imparts the necessary spiritual gifts to them, at the moment these gifts are needed. The purpose of the gifts, and the powerful encounters they generate, are meant to meet the need of the unbeliever in confirmation of the Word that is being proclaimed.

Praying in the Spirit

In addition to power to witness to unbelievers, Spirit-baptism also provides divine power in the personal prayer life of the believer. All Christians can pray and be personally edified in their known human language. However, when a person has been baptized with the Holy Spirit, a new prayer dimension is made available called, "praying in the Spirit."

In 1 Corinthians 14, the Apostle Paul is contextually instructing the Corinthian believers in the corporate use of tongues. In verse 2, he explains,

> *...anyone who speaks in a tongue does not speak to people but to God. Indeed, no one understands them; they utter mysteries by the Spirit.*[93]

It is important to understand that when one speaks in tongues, the words the speaker is using are not understood. It is the inability to understand what is being said that makes the speaking "mysterious." The person speaking is speaking by the Spirit. In verse 14, Paul says,

> *For if I pray in a tongue, my spirit prays, but my mind is unfruitful.*

He is again acknowledging that when a person prays in tongues, the person's spirit is praying, even though the person's mind does not understand the exact words being spoken. In verse 4, Paul is careful to note that while a person speaking in tongues does not understand the actual words he or she is using, that person is still being edified.

The Apostle asks the question in verse 15, *"So what shall I do?"* and then answers his own question by saying, *"I will pray with my spirit, but I will also pray with my mind."* Paul is saying, that he will pray in tongues, and he will pray using his own human language.

This is what Paul is explaining in Romans 8:26-27, when he talks about praying with groans that words cannot express:

> *In the same way, the Spirit helps us in our weakness. We do not know what we ought to pray for, but the Spirit himself intercedes for us through wordless groans. And he who searches our hearts knows the mind of the Spirit,*

---

[93] 1 Corinthians 14:2.

because the Spirit intercedes for God's people in accordance with the will of God.[94]

Often, believers pray in their known language and still remain burdened for a particular need, but do not know what else to do. It is at that point that praying in tongues provides divine enablement. The believer, burdened for non-Christian friends, family, or co-workers, begins to pray for them in tongues. As the individual does so, it is the Holy Spirit that is interceding, through the Spirit-baptized believer, in accordance with the will of God.

I believe every time Paul uses the phrase "pray in the spirit" he is always referring to praying in tongues. For example, in Ephesians 6:18-20, he encourages the Ephesians to "pray in the spirit on all occasions." Then he also encourages them to pray for specific requests he gave them. So he is exhorting the Ephesians to pray in the spirit (to pray in tongues), but also to pray in their own languages for those specific requests.

And pray in the Spirit on all occasions with all kinds of prayers and requests. With this in mind, be alert and always keep on praying for all the Lord's people. Pray also for me, that whenever I speak, words may be given me so that I will fearlessly make known the mystery of the gospel, for which I am an ambassador in chains. Pray that I may declare it fearlessly, as I should.[95]

In the book of Jude, the author produced a long list of the characteristics of false teachers, unbelievers, and ungodly people who were coming into the church causing trouble and division. He compared them to ungodly people from the past

---

[94] Romans 8:26-27.
[95] Ephesians 6:18-20.

upon whom God had brought judgment, and predicted a similar condemnation for them. In light of this conflict and opposition, Jude encouraged his readers to keep themselves in the love of God by building themselves up in their most holy faith and *"praying in the Holy Spirit."*[96] Linking edification in the faith and praying in the Spirit, Jude echoes the Apostle Paul's instructions in 1 Corinthians 14. Jude expected his readers to remain in the love of God by building themselves up in the faith and by praying in tongues.

How to be Spirit-Baptized

Many people have asked me the question: "How can a person be baptized with the Holy Spirit?" The answer is found in Luke 11:13,

> *If you then, though you are evil, know how to give good gifts to your children, how much more will your Father in heaven give the Holy Spirit to those who ask him!*

Here Luke instructs his readers to pray, asking for the gift of the Holy Spirit. Let me quickly insert here: the request is for the Holy Spirit, and more specifically, for the *baptism* with the Holy Spirit. The request is *not* for the gift of tongues, or the ability to speak in tongues.

According to John the Baptist's prophecy, it is Jesus Christ who baptizes people with the Holy Spirit. Therefore, it is reasonable for those who want to be baptized with the Spirit to ask *Jesus* to baptize them. Let Jesus know you want to be empowered to be His witness to the lost.

If this experience does not happen the first time you ask, do not stop asking. Continue to believe and continue to ask until you are baptized with the Spirit. You will know when you are,

---

[96] Jude 20-21.

because you will speak in other tongues as the Spirit enables you.

Spirit Baptism and Military Ministry

So how does all of this impact our ministry to young military men and women?

First of all, these young warriors put their lives at risk for the freedoms and values of our country and for people around the world. They need to hear the gospel message, and be introduced to Jesus Christ. As I mentioned before, the most effective means of evangelizing military personnel is through other military personnel—*insiders*. Therefore, we need to help young Christian military men and women receive the empowerment of the Holy Spirit to make them the most effective and powerful witnesses they can be in the military environment.

A great deal of pressure exists against being Christ-centered and evangelistic in the military community. This will probably only increase in coming years. Accusations of being intolerant and insensitive are frequently used to describe (and neutralize) Christians who try to share their faith with others, no matter how sensitively these attempts are made. But this does not change the mandate for Christians to be witnesses for Christ. As a result, it is necessary for these young people to be supernaturally empowered as witnesses for Jesus Christ in a potentially hostile environment. This includes standing for Him and being a clear and articulate witness, even in the face of ridicule, opposition, and persecution. God has provided this divine power through the baptism with the Holy Spirit.

In our 18 years of ministry with the military in Virginia Beach there have been 9 servicemen and women who have been received the baptism with the Holy Spirit. Some while they were here with us and others after they were transferred to other locations.

You Shared the Holy Spirit with Me

In addition to the marine I mentioned at the beginning of this chapter, there were two sailors who were baptized with the Holy Spirit in 2001 that I want to mention. The first was a quiet and reserved young man, who was really into martial arts. He was about to be transferred to a ship in Japan. Not long before he left, he was baptized with the Holy Spirit and called us to let us know. He told us, when he got to his ship, he wanted to be a "Ninja for Christ."

The other young sailor also called us when he was baptized with the Holy Spirit. Immediately, he began sharing his faith in Jesus Christ with his shipmates to the point where many of them began asking him if he was going to become a "preacher." I'll say more about both of these young men in the next chapter.

10

YOU HELPED ME SHARE MY FAITH

One of the key objectives in our ministry is to help servicemen and women become culturally sensitive witnesses for Jesus Christ among military personnel in their units, among multinational forces when they are engaged in combined military operations, and among civilian residents of the countries where they may serve. Because the military environment is so restrictive, Christian servicemen and women who have been empowered, trained, and encouraged to share their faith make the best witnesses to other military men and women. They are "insiders" who have the most direct access to other American service personnel

The same is true when Christian servicemen and women from our country are stationed together with the military personnel of other nations in combined military operations. And when they are stationed in other countries, they have direct access to, and are able to interact with, the citizens of those countries. As a result, they can be significant ambassadors of the gospel of Jesus Christ throughout the world.

You Invited Me In...

It's been exciting to see individuals who have been involved in our ministry share their faith in Christ with other servicemen and women in their units, even in the face of opposition. It has also been exciting to hear the stories of how they shared their faith with military personnel of other countries while in combined service environments, and how they shared their faith with civilian residents of countries where they visited or were stationed. Let me share some stories with you. I've omitted any personally identifying information to respect their privacy.

Military Personnel in Their Own Units

I'll begin with three young men who shared their faith with other personnel in their own units. The first story concerns a young sailor stationed aboard a submarine in Groton, Connecticut, who participated in our ministry activities while in Virginia Beach on a temporary duty assignment. While he was here, we studied my book, *How to Become a More Effective Personal Witness*. He asked if we would help him train Christians on his submarine to be more effective witnesses for Christ. His plan was to start a training course using my book. We agreed, and after he finished his training here, he went back to his submarine in Groton, taking one of my books with him.

He sent us the following email: "I was wondering if you have any more of those *How to Become a More Effective Personal Witness* workbooks. I recently lent my copy to a sailor on one of the other submarines and foresee needing more copies in the future. Let me know where I can get some and how much they cost.

He went on to explain: "I am trying to start a sort of ministry to the lay leaders in Groton, CT. I see a need for their training and encouragement toward an effective small-group meeting while underway, and also the need for fellowship between the leaders and their groups while in port.

"So I have been talking to the lay leaders, the chaplains, and my pastors to get this thing moving. Last week, I invited four lay leaders to meet me at *Chile's* for dinner so I could talk with them about their specific needs for ministry. For one reason or another, no lay leaders showed up, but the leader on one of the other submarines sent one of the guys in his group in his stead. So, it was just me and [him] last night. We had a good time talking about a range of topics in relation to the small group on his boat.

"[He] mentioned his attempts at witnessing to some people on his boat, and I immediately thought of the workbook you gave me. So I lent it to him and he will be studying it."

Yvonne and I responded to his request and sent him ten books (at no cost).

The second story is about the young sailor I mentioned earlier who said he wanted to be a "Ninja for Christ." He received orders to a ship homeported in Yokosuka, Japan. But before leaving the Norfolk-Virginia Beach area, he attended a ministers' meeting with Yvonne and me and shared his personal testimony with the local pastors. That was quite a big step for him!

Later, after arriving aboard his ship in Japan, he emailed us about his experiences trying to witness to his shipmates: "I have made it known that I am a Christian to most, if not all, of the people in my division; now because of this I know that they are watching me. It seems as though many of the guys here say that they too were once self-proclaimed "altar boys", but that I would break.

"One shipmate was especially amused at me and tried to ask me tough questions....challenging me in my belief, trying to make what I believe not make sense.

"I told him that I have a personal relationship with Jesus Christ. [He] looked at me like he wanted to laugh and then asked: 'Has he asked about me?'

You Invited Me In…

"I figured he was making a joke at me, so I responded "No, not lately."

"But here is the cool part: after that first encounter I later asked him, "What caused you to break? I mean, you said 'I haven't talked to him in a long time,' which must mean you used to have faith."

"He answered, "Well after a while, everything I believed started to not make sense out here (in the fleet, out to sea in foreign ports), and I just gave up" (that isn't a direct quote).

"Later, (earlier today) he asked, 'so, have you crucified anyone today?'

"I told him Christians are more about being compassion and forgiving as they are forgiven, rather than taking a high and mighty righteous position, and that a lot of people claim to be Christian, but really are not.

"Then we had a brief discussion about how being a Christian is about that personal relationship with Jesus, through prayer and Bible study, not so much about going to church. (He told me about a time at school when a priest was really "accusational" when people weren't coming to church every Sunday).

"MORAL OF MY STORY IS:

"I think [he] is being drawn toward me, to talk about God, Jesus, and Christianity, and maybe I am one of the workers of the harvest in his life. He reminds me of the way Saul was on a much less dramatic scale. Persecutor to possible follower, and friend. Give me a BIG WOOOOOOHOOOOOO!!!! YEAHHH!!! GOOOO JESUS.

"Extra: I recalled when he asked if Jesus had asked about him. And at first, I didn't realize it, but now I <u>know</u> that yes, Jesus has indeed been asking me about [him].

"I have to be careful and let him approach me with a cynical question to start the conversation, or he might totally turn on listening to me. Either way, the battle between good and evil is now in him."

You Helped Me Share My Faith

Our young "ninja" tried starting a Bible study on his ship, but things didn't go well. He sent us an email detailing some of the frustrations he was experiencing:

"I am afraid that my Bible study with my friend has yet to begin. We both have busy working schedules, and the only time available is when I am asleep, or when she is asleep. I was willing to forfeit some sleep to make the Bible study happen, but when my partner finally got done working, she went to bed, really tired. I went to bed after a while. I have been continuing to ask people if they have a faith, and if they believe the contents of the Bible.

"I have a list of 5 people who I am targeting to invite to the Bible study. They say they are Roman Catholic, Lutheran, and one guy who I asked his faith said, 'I'll go with Christian.'

"Then I rephrased the question to... "Do you believe the contents of the Bible?"

He said "Yes."

And I said, "That's a good start" with a smile."

Our young "Ninja" also frequently reported that, although he attempted to share his faith in Christ as much as possible, he faced some significant opposition. He wrote and said: "Shipmates are trying to corrupt me still. Last night, I went to put my Bible under my pillow, and I found what they call a "training magazine." It was pornography. I went in the head [restroom] and casually tore it in half. I made sure that they knew that I did it too. They won't be likely to "waste" any more of that stuff by making it available to me...Take care and fight the good fight."

At times, Yvonne and I could hear by the things he said, and the tone of his emails, that the pressure presented by his shipmates often seemed unrelenting and overwhelming. He wrote: "I am feeling truly tried in my walk with God lately. I am aware that by professing my faith to my shipmates, I have set myself up as a target. It is tough. They are determined to try to

You Invited Me In...

make me doubt myself and God, make me compromise what I think and know. I have been resistant so far, but I realize that I am being challenged.

"Then I also realized that I hadn't read my Bible over the last 2 nights, and that I needed to. I opened it and was thinking of needing some inspiration for perseverance. Well as soon as I started reading, Halleluiah! I read Romans Chapter 12. All of it.

"It was a help, I felt soothed of my trials, and that I can go on without being changed for the worse.

"All of my shipmates say, 'Trust me, you'll change.'

"I am in prayer for my solidness of faith through tribulation, may it give me grace, and stronger faith. I love you all. Miss you."

Thus, a quiet, shy young man was emboldened by the power of the Holy Spirit to be a witness for Jesus Christ on his ship, even in the face of considerable personal pressure and opposition.

The third story is about the young sailor I mentioned earlier who accepted Jesus Christ in a local restaurant as a result of Yvonne's sharing the four spiritual laws with him. The story begins with his going home on Christmas leave and witnessing to several of his high school friends. He ended up leading his best friend to faith in Jesus Christ.

In the spring of the following year, after being baptized with the Holy Spirit, his boldness increased. He attended a ministers' fellowship in the Norfolk-Virginia Beach area with Yvonne and me and shared his testimony with several local pastors. And then, shared his testimony again from the pulpit during a Protestant worship service in the chapel at Oceana Naval Air Station.

A few months later, he approached me with a passionate desire to again share his faith in Christ with his friends back home. He wanted to plan, promote, and conduct a revival service among the teens in his home town. We thought it was a great idea and encouraged and supported his efforts. In addition, he sought the counsel of two other local pastors. One of them, after conferring with us, agreed to support his efforts and provided some financial resources for the endeavor.

The other pastor was reluctant to encourage him in the venture, and went so far as to give him several reasons why he should not proceed. One of his reasons was that the project lacked "pastoral oversight." The young man came to me dejected, discouraged and confused. I reassured him that he *was* in fact functioning under "pastoral oversight" – ours. He decided to move forward with his plan, went back to the pastor, and assured him he *was* functioning under pastoral oversight – ours. After receiving that assurance, that pastor also provided encouragement and some financial resources for the project.

The young man wrote a letter of introduction to the pastors of 300 churches within an hour's drive of his home town, explaining what he wanted to do, and inviting their youth to the revival. In his youthful exuberance, denominational differences meant nothing!

He rented a middle school auditorium in his home town as the venue for the revival. And, realizing he would need music for the event, hired the associate minister of music of a local Norfolk church to play the keyboard and sing. He went so far as to purchase a round trip airline ticket for her.

He also bought a keyboard and sound amplification system for the event out of his own personal funds. Finally, he took leave from the Navy to conduct the revival.

Three churches in the area participated in his event, with 22 high school students in attendance. Two of the teens invited Jesus Christ into their lives, and one recommitted her life to Christ. After the revival service, a youth pastor from a church in the area whose young people had not attended the revival, invited him to speak to their youth group the following night. Eight high school students attended that event.

You Invited Me In...

We were all really excited about the results of his revival meeting! It seems God's call rests on this young man's life. With his passion and enthusiasm for the Lord, and his organizational skills, it seems there are great things in store for his future.

Shortly afterward, his orders were cut short in the Norfolk-Virginia Beach area and he was transferred to a ship in Italy. While there, he stayed in contact with us through emails and telephone calls and communicated regularly about his efforts to share his faith in Christ with his shipmates. He said several of them suggested he become a "preacher" because he was so convincing in his presentation of the gospel.

Combined Military Operations

Two stories come to mind in the area of witnessing to military men and women in a combined military operations setting. The first involves the young marine who was so excited about being baptized with the Holy Spirit when he returned from Christmas leave.

After finishing his training in our area he received orders to Okinawa, Japan. And while stationed there, was sent on a temporary duty assignment to Korea, for guard duty. He told us that while in Korea, he shared his faith in Christ with some of the Korean guards who were working with him.

He described what happened in an email saying: "I just recently returned from Korea. It was really cool interacting with the Korean guards and making friends. It was cool to share the Word with some of them too. I had a Korean/English Bible, so I was able to do so." Only God knows what the spiritual outcome of that encounter will be.

The second story involves Yvonne and me and the Brazilian ship that came to Norfolk for combined Naval training operations that I mentioned in Chapter 5.

The story began when Yvonne and I received the email from Rubem, in Rio de Janeiro. He stayed in touch with us during the months before they arrived, sending us an email every month to make sure we didn't forget about him.

When the ship pulled into port, Yvonne and I were pier side, carrying the sign with his name. After the ship tied up to the pier, we were escorted aboard and met him. The only problem was he did not speak English, and Yvonne and I don't speak Portuguese.

He introduced us to a friend of his who spoke a little English. So we were able to communicate some, but with great difficulty. Then they had to go back to work. We finalized plans to come back at the end of their work day to pick Rubem up for dinner.

I tried getting someone from Regent University who spoke Portuguese to translate for us. But no one was available. So I went to Barnes and Nobles and bought a Portuguese/English dictionary.

When Yvonne and I returned to the ship later that evening, we met Rubem and *four* friends. He asked if they could all come for dinner. Our response was, "Of Course!" None of them spoke much English, so we used a lot of hand gestures, pointed, and laughed a lot.

Yvonne made a big pot of her homemade spaghetti sauce and pasta, and homemade bread. I discovered at dinner that the sailors actually could understand English fairly well, and that some of them could speak English better than they professed. It was just a matter of getting over the fear of speaking a newly acquired language and making a mistake.

We enjoyed learning to communicate with each other. But occasionally didn't know how to get an idea across so we would open the dictionary and look up the necessary words. After a while whenever we needed to do that someone would say, "The book! The book!" One of the men said pronouncing English words made him feel "Batata Na Boca" - like he had a "Potato in the mouth."

The men joined our activities every weekend their ship was in port and they didn't have duty. One Saturday morning, one of

You Invited Me In...

our regular sailors picked the Brazilians up at their ship and took them shopping all day for gifts for their wives and children. Afterward, they came back to our house for dinner, and we all went to Harbor Park to watch the Brazilians' first-ever American baseball game. On subsequent weekends, we went miniature golfing and bowling together, played croquet in our back yard, and put puzzles together.

The spiritual highlight of our weekends with them were our worship services on Sunday. One of the Brazilian sailors brought and played his flute, while another played the guitar. We sang choruses and songs we all knew. The Brazilians would sing them in Portuguese and the rest of us would sing them in English.

We watched the *Matthew* DVD video series (in Spanish with English subtitles). They said they could actually understand it. After watching the video I would explain a passage in English, one of the guys would translate it into Portuguese, and then they would discuss it among themselves in Portuguese. Two of the Brazilian sailors recommitted their lives to Jesus Christ while they were with us.

One particular Sunday afternoon, instead of having everyone watch the Matthew video, I talked about what was happening between us. The love we felt for each other in such a short time was nothing short of divine! Jesus' sacrifice on the Cross and His Resurrection made this all possible.

I pointed out that we were all sharing our gifts with one another. Two of the sailors were sharing their gifts of music. Yvonne and I were sharing our gifts of cooking and hospitality. Jesus said He came that we might have life and have it to the full.[97] By coming together, fellowshipping and loving one another as we were, we were tasting a little bit of what He meant!

We sang the chorus, *"Open The Eyes of My Heart"* several times. We all felt like we were "seeing" Jesus. He made it

---

[97] John 10:10.

You Helped Me Share My Faith

possible for six sailors from Brazil to come to the United States and share their gift of music and their love with us in our home. Jesus also made it possible for us—a man and woman in the United States—to open our home and love six sailors from Brazil. In just four short weeks, He made it possible for us to love each other deeply from the heart. After sharing my thoughts, we went back to singing. It was great!

We knew that the Brazilians' stay in America was coming to a close, so after we sang some more, we all stood up. I anointed each one of them individually with oil in the name of the Lord Jesus, and prayed for them.

On another Sunday afternoon while we worshipped together, I celebrated Holy Communion as all of us knelt on the floor around our coffee table. After our time of worship, their newly acquired laptops came out and they began calling home on Skype. All of the sailors wanted to introduce Yvonne and me to their families in Brazil.

Rubem called his mother and introduced us. His mother spoke to us and thanked us for our hospitality, and then began humming a hymn we recognized. So we all began singing it together—Yvonne and I in English and the Brazilian sailors in Portuguese.

Rubem's mother also asked us to pray for his God-father who was having surgery on a tumor in his leg. We began praying and the Holy Spirit filled the room. What started out as a simple prayer turned into an old fashioned Holy Ghost prayer meeting that spanned two continents! We prayed in human languages – English and Portuguese. And we prayed in angelic languages – glossolalia.[98] What a powerful presence of the Holy Spirit filled our living room that night!

A couple of weeks later, the Brazilian ship was scheduled to head back to its homeport. Yvonne and I again went to the pier

---

[98] 1 Corinthians 13:1

You Invited Me In...

and waved to our new "sons" as we watched them pull out of the harbor.

Civilian Residents of the Countries Where They Serve

Christian servicemen and women are also powerful witnesses among the residents of the countries where they are stationed. An excellent example of this is the story I just shared. The Christian sailors aboard the Brazilian ship that came here had been powerful witnesses to Yvonne and me. And as a result of our combined efforts to play, worship, and glorify God together, two of their shipmates recommitted their lives to Jesus Christ while in our home.

Let me also go back to our young "ninja" and continue his story. The young man's ship went on deployment to Australia. While there, he emailed us and shared some of his witnessing experiences:

He said, "I have to tell you about a friend I met in Australia... [We] pulled into Darwin, Australia....We went on liberty into town, where I ran into 3 shipmates and wandered around with them...

"We went to this little Internet Cafe called "Byte Me." There one shipmate and I played chess... [I also met the waitress who worked in the café].

"Next day I was out with...a good shipmate, he is supportive of my faith and isn't trying to tempt me.

"I was by a phone booth and [the waitress from the café] and her brother walked by.

"I said 'Hi,' and they stopped and talked to me.

"By the end of the conversation I was going to a movie with [her] and her brother...

"After the movie, [she] invited me to her house...and I had dinner with them....

"She asked me why I joined the Navy... I kept [the conversation] up with long detailed drawn out answers. I also had the chance to witness to her that evening....

"I spent almost the whole weekend seeing Darwin, Australia... [with them]. The whole time I was able to talk with them about America, the US Navy, and Christianity....

"We are really good friends in a short time. I talked to [her] about God and Jesus...

"She isn't a Christian, she doesn't even agree with some of the Bible, but she is open to discussion, and I am trying to show her the truth....

"And her brother is even more open to the word. He says he is Catholic, but he seems to not really know the specifics of Catholic belief. And [she] tells me that from what he believes, he is more inclined to be a Christian, if he is shown what being a Christian is about. That is where I want to come in and help...."

Yvonne and I were so pleased to hear how bold this young sailor had become in sharing his faith in Christ. He shared with his shipmates, even in the face of opposition, and with the residents of countries where his ship went.

There is also more to the story of our young "preacher" who was transferred to Italy. His ship went into dry dock in Malta. While there, he attended a local Spirit-filled Maltese church, and became actively involved in their worship service. One of the church's electric guitars broke and the congregation could not afford to purchase a new one, so he ordered one for them as a gift out of his own finances.

We believe this young man's zeal and enthusiasm for sharing his faith in Jesus Christ with his family and friends in his home town was divinely inspired. His desire and ability to share his faith with his shipmates is also an indication of the divine power at work within him. And his love and desire to be a witness to the people of Malta is still further evidence of the power he received when he was baptized with the Holy Spirit.

You Invited Me In...

Our last story is about the young soldier I mentioned earlier who invited Jesus Christ into his life on the Thanksgiving Day when the crew of the Coast Guard cutter did not join us.

After finishing his training here, he received orders to Germany. While there, he got involved with one of our Ministry to the Military centers. He attended services there regularly, and even participated in their Vacation Bible School one summer—portraying one of the biblical characters in a Bible skit for the children of military personnel and local Germans.

These six stories are examples of what the Holy Spirit can accomplish through servicemen and women who commit their lives to Jesus Christ as their Savior, are discipled in their new faith, receive divine power to be witnesses for Jesus Christ through the baptism with the Holy Spirit, and who are then trained and encouraged to share their faith with other servicemen and women in their military units, among multinational forces in combined military operations, and among civilian residents of countries where they get sent.

Christian military men and women can become significant ambassadors of the gospel of Jesus Christ throughout the world. And *you* can have a significant global impact for Jesus Christ right from your living room by inviting them in...

11

YOU DIDN'T FORGET ME!

As we bring our story to a close, I want to talk about one of the most important aspects of our ministry to the military: maintaining contact. For Yvonne and me, ministering to young military men and women is more than just ministering to them as long as they are stationed here. It is about building lasting relationships with them and investing in their lives—an investment that lasts well beyond their assignment in our local area.

We tell all of the servicemen and women who come into our home that after their first visit, we "adopt" them and consider them to be part of our extended family. For us, that is more than just a nice sentiment. It is something we mean sincerely from the depths of our hearts.

As I said earlier in our story, everything starts with providing a safe and caring home and family environment for servicemen and women. We work to meet them through a variety of ways, and invite them into our home. Then through the activities we participate in together, we get to know them and build personal relationships with them.

You Invited Me In…

After all the effort we expend to connect with these young people, we do everything we can to maintain our connection with them as they travel throughout this country and around the world. Maintaining those relationships has enabled us to continue ministering in their lives even after they left Virginia—and even after they have gotten out of the military.

One of the things Yvonne and I had to learn to deal with early in this ministry was the "irregularity" of servicemen and women's duty schedules, and the highly transient nature of military life as a whole. Both of these realities made ministering to these young men and women difficult. We wanted them to be in attendance at all of our activities every week, but that was impossible because of their tightly regulated duty schedules. We had to learn and accept that their attendance would be sporadic at best.

In spite of their irregular attendance, we still need to reach out to them. They still need to hear the gospel message. And they still need to be loved and cared for. Ministering to servicemen and women cannot be about trying to build a stable growing church, or about building measurable, increasing numbers in the groups attending our activities. Staying connected with them as much as possible in spite of their transient schedules is essential for ongoing, lasting, ministry into their lives. And all of this takes significant time, effort, and investment.

Let me share two conversations I had with two different pastors to illustrate my point. Though similar in content, these two conversations were separated by 30 years.

The first one occurred when I was 20 years old, and stationed in the Navy in Hawaii. I was an enthusiastic young Christian and attending a local Pentecostal church. With thousands of people in the army, navy, and air force stationed in the area, I wondered why our church wasn't doing anything to reach out to them. So one day, I asked the pastor. I'll never forget his response.

You Didn't Forget Me!

He said that reaching the military was hard. And after reaching them, they don't stay around very long. As soon as a serviceman comes into the church and gets actively involved, he or she gets deployed for months at a time, or gets transferred away. That leaves huge holes in the ministry positions of the church.

As a result, he said, we can't build a stable, growing church on the military community. The focus of our church has to be on the more "stable" civilian population. He must have noticed the shocked expression on my face, because he quickly tried to reassure me that military people were "welcome" to attend our church and worship with us. But our ministry efforts would not focus on them directly.

Thirty years later, Yvonne and I had moved to Virginia Beach to minister to the military. We attended a military ministry conference in Kings Bay, Georgia. Looking for a church to attend on Sunday morning, we found a local Pentecostal church near the base that even advertised a "military ministry." Our interest was piqued so we attended their worship service.

We enjoyed the service, and afterward introduced ourselves to the pastor and his wife, and asked them about their military ministry. Sadly, he said, they didn't have one anymore. Two years earlier, they had a thriving military ministry with 54 people actively involved. Many of them served in key leadership positions in the church.

He explained that suddenly, with little warning, the Navy transferred one of the submarines, its crew, and their families from Kings Bay to Bremerton, Washington. And of course, it just so happened that most of the people involved in the church's military ministry were from *that* submarine. The pastor said it decimated their military ministry, and almost destroyed the church. Two years later, they were still struggling to recover from the negative impact that move created.

You Invited Me In...

The pastor and church were understandably discouraged! They tried to minister to the military with the understanding that they would be there permanently. They counted on the sailors and their families being part of the church services and church community every week. When that didn't happen because of the Navy's operational changes, the church's desire to minister to the military evaporated.

I wanted to try to encourage the pastor, and asked if I could offer him a different perspective. He agreed, and I began by asking him some questions:

I asked, "What if God purposely brought the people from that submarine to his church, for the brief time they were going to be there, for their church to prepare them for their next assignment?"

I went on to ask, "What if the things he and his church gave those sailors and their families were things they wouldn't have gotten at any other church?"

And, "What if the things they received from their church made them better Christians, better church members, better Sunday school teachers, better witnesses, and better leaders than they were before they came to their church?"

He said he had never thought about that possibility. I went on to suggest that, because of the transient nature of the military community, and the small size of the submarine force specifically, there was a very good possibility that some of the people from that submarine could get transferred back to their area in the future for duty on a different submarine. I suggested it might be a good idea to stay in touch with them to let them know that they were still loved and cared for by the church and that they were welcome to come back.

After all, I explained, it wasn't their fault they were transferred. And the move was probably as traumatic for them as it was for the church. If the church maintained the relationships they developed with these sailors and their families by sending cards and letters, exchanging telephone calls and emails, when they returned to their area they would be far more likely to come back to the church, than if they felt they had been cut off, cast aside, and forgotten.

The pastor and his wife seemed genuinely appreciative of my comments. And seemed encouraged by the possibility of staying in touch with the families who had been transferred away.

Both of these pastors were intimidated and overwhelmed by the transient nature of the military. The first to the point where he would not even attempt to intentionally reach out to them. The second was so hurt by the military's transient nature that he had given up on reaching out to them.

The end result?

In both situations young men and women in the military were not being ministered to, nor being intentionally reached with the gospel of Jesus Christ. Both pastors were willing to have servicemen and women attend their churches and worship with their congregations, if *they* sought the churches out and came *to them*. However, with 80 percent of young adults between the ages of 18 and 30 being indifferent to God, religion, and church, that was probably not going to happen.

So let me share the various ways Yvonne and I have attempted to maintain contact with the servicemen and women who have been in our home throughout the years.

Regular Duty Schedules

During the first few years of our ministry here our primary method of communication with soldiers, sailors, and marines was through emails and telephone calls. But, with the advent and popularity of new technology and social media, this has changed. Facebook is now our principle method of staying in touch with them.

You Invited Me In...

Yvonne and I post descriptions of our weekend ministry activities, some personal and family events, and scripture passages, prayer requests, songs, poems, and pictures on our Facebook wall. These posts let the servicemen keep in touch with us and our ministry activities. As I've said, I take lots of pictures during our weekend activities and post them on Facebook. When I tag the ones who participate, their friends and extended family members see what we (and they) are doing.

Soldiers, sailors, marines, and airmen post their personal activities and pictures on their Facebook walls. So by visiting their walls Yvonne and I keep up with what is going on in their lives, post comments in response to the things they write, and post our own messages of encouragement to them.

With the advent of cell phones, we have another vital tool that lets us stay in touch with our adopted sons and daughters. Texting has clearly become the preferred method of communicating with most young adults today. Sending a text message gets an almost immediate response. This is why we find our guest book pages invaluable! With them, we have a permanent record of names and cell phone numbers.

When we initially receive the name and phone number of potential new service members who might be interested in attending our activities, Yvonne will call them, introduce herself, and invite them to the house. After that, she will text them regularly, to repeat the invitation. Once they have been to the house, Yvonne will text them each week to find out if they are coming over to join us for our weekend activities. This gives her an idea of how much food to purchase and prepare for our meals. Other times, she will text them simply to find out how their day or week is going.

We also keep in touch spiritually. Yvonne and I pray regularly for every serviceman and woman that comes to our home, lifting them up before the Lord in our personal devotional times. Much of what military men and women do in their daily jobs can be extremely dangerous. So we ask God to watch over them and protect them. We also ask the Lord to draw those who don't believe to Him, and to keep those who do, close to Him. We ask God to help them resist the temptations they are sure to confront. If the young man or woman is a Christian, we ask the Lord to give him or her opportunities to share the love of Jesus and the gospel message with shipmates.

Short-Term Duty Assignments

Normal life for a man or woman in the military involves both scheduled and unscheduled short-term duty assignments in remote places. These assignments can last from a few days to several weeks, and even a few months.

How we stay in touch with our soldiers, sailors, marines or airmen when they go on short-term duty assignments depends on where they go, what their job is, and what level of security is involved in their assignment. The most important thing Yvonne and I try to keep in mind is not to forget them when they're gone. The old adage, "Out of sight, out of mind." really comes into play here. When a serviceman or woman leaves, life goes on pretty much like normal here. And the time they are gone goes by very quickly. So we have to make intentional and concerted efforts to maintain contact.

For several years, I sent a weekly email of encouragement to all of the men and women involved in our ministry. These emails included descriptions of our weekend activities, and a short devotional. It was designed to be a way of staying in touch with them and helping them feel like they were still part of our fellowship. Facebook posts have largely replaced that weekly email. They are shorter, can include pictures, and can be accessed from almost anywhere they are.

Again, we maintain our spiritual connection with them while they are away by praying for each serviceman and woman in our personal devotional times. We also pray for them as a group in our prayer times during our weekend activities.

Extended Deployments

Maintaining contact with our adopted sons and daughters while they are on extended deployments is similar to keeping in touch with them while they're on short-term assignments—with a few specific differences. Our experience in maintaining contact with them on deployment has mostly been with sailors on ships serving in the Middle East, and with marines and soldiers in combat settings in Afghanistan and Iraq. These deployments vary significantly in length. Naval deployments are generally 6 to 9 months long. Marines usually deploy for 12 months. While soldiers are deployed anywhere from one year to 18 months.

One of the first things Yvonne and I do when our sailors go on deployment is go to the pier to see them off. And, when they come back, we are again pier side to greet them and welcome them home. Sometimes the sailor's parents come from out of state to see the ship off, or meet it when it comes back. When we are on the pier together, it gives us a chance to meet and get to know them.

Again, Facebook is our primary method of staying in touch. As when they go on short-term assignments, while they are deployed, they continue posting their activities on their Facebook walls. Yvonne and I visit their walls to look at the pictures of the exotic places they visit and read the stories they post. And, we respond and post messages of our own to them.

Because deployments are much longer, one of Yvonne's favorite ways to stay in touch is by sending "care packages." She puts together goodies she's baked and small items (like games, puzzles and cards) in the boxes. These packages are meant to let them know they are still cared for and remembered.

Using our guest book pages, Yvonne keeps track of their birthdays and wedding anniversaries. She sends cards and small gifts to help them commemorate those special days.

We also maintain our website and blog, two other ways we keep in touch. We post all kinds of pictures of our activities there, along with articles and Bible studies I've written. We discuss and answer questions, address issues the articles may raise as they read them, and do Bible studies by email.

Once again, we maintain our spiritual connection while they are on deployment by lifting them up before the Lord in our personal prayer times and during our weekend activities. We always ask God to watch over them and protect them. And we continue to pray that God will use the Christians to be His witnesses to their shipmates, to military men and women from other countries, and among the people of the countries where they make port visits.

Permanent Duty Station Changes

Eventually, we come to the time when we have to say "good-bye," because a soldier, sailor, or marine receives orders transferring him or her to a new duty station. His departure may take him to another part of our country, or another part of the world. Saying goodbye is always hard. Because we focus on establishing close personal relationships with those who come into our home, when they leave, it's like saying good-bye to our own son or daughter.

We know there is always the possibility that, if she stays in the military, she will be transferred back to our area. So we do everything we can to ensure the relationships we've established continue. But even if they don't get sent back to this area, our love for them doesn't end—any more than our love and concern for our biological children ends when they grow up and move away. We believe that our spiritual responsibility to the young men and women who have been in our home continues. It takes

You Invited Me In...

time and effort to stay in touch, but it is worth it in the long run because it enables us to continue ministering to their spiritual needs.

One example of this was our young "Ninja for Christ" whose experiences I shared in the last chapter. When he received orders to a ship in Japan, I told him we would consider him our "representative" on his ship. He liked that idea and stayed in touch with us through emails and telephone calls. He emailed us regularly, telling us about his experiences on the ship. Occasionally he called us on the telephone when he got into a port, to let us know how he was doing, and to tell us about his efforts at sharing Christ with his shipmates.

This young sailor's experiences are not uncommon, and are why we believe it is so important to keep in touch with them. The enemy of their souls will attempt to do all he can to try to destroy them. As with the men and women who go on deployment, Yvonne and I pray regularly for those who are transferred to new duty stations.

Early in our ministry in Virginia Beach, Yvonne searched online for Pentecostal servicemen's centers overseas. She found that the Church of God had a ministry to the military and operated Pentecostal servicemen's centers in Europe and Asia. So we began recommending these centers to the young men and women who were transferring away from here. She also began contacting the center directors to let them know that one of our adopted "sons" or "daughters" were coming their way. This was how we initially became associated with the Church of God.

So when the other young sailor I mentioned in the last chapter was transferred to Gaeta, Italy, Yvonne got in contact with Kaye and Owen Martin, the center directors there. And we recommended he contact them. When he arrived he received a warm welcome at their center, and found his Pentecostal beliefs nurtured and strengthened.

You Didn't Forget Me!

Later, when his ship went into the shipyard on Malta for repairs, Yvonne found the San Gwann Assembly of God on Malta through the International Assemblies of God website. She emailed Pastor Ahmed Bugri, and told him about our young sailor, and emailed our sailor and told him about the church. When he arrived in Malta, he was greeted by the pastor and the church with open arms.

When the young soldier I told you about received orders to Wiesbaden, Germany, Yvonne got in touch with Ken and Sharon Gallion, the directors of the Wiesbaden Christian Servicemen's Center, again operated by the Church of God. Our soldier got involved in their fellowship and helped minister to the children of military families during their summer Vacation Bible School program.

We try, as much as possible, to be involved in the special events of these young people's lives. Most notably this is when they get married. Yvonne and I are often invited to participate in or officiate at their weddings.

In addition to staying in touch through emails, telephone calls, and text messages, we also maintain our connections with our sons and daughters by visiting them at their new duty stations. Yvonne and I frequently attend military ministry conferences that are held in various parts of the country. And whenever we do, we drive to where they are held. This gives us the opportunity to visit the servicemen and women who have been in our home along the way.

Permanently Separating from the Military

Finally, the time comes when most of the servicemen and women who came through our home leave the service permanently. Many get out of the military to go to college, to get married and start a family, or simply get out because they have come to the end of their obligated time of service and have decided they no longer want to stay in the military. Whatever the reason, when they do "take off the uniform for the last time," Yvonne and I try to maintain our relationship with them.

Sometimes a former serviceman or woman will contact us for help in witnessing to a friend or family member. One former soldier wrote for help witnessing to a friend. She said,

> "I'm home now in California. I can't find that little book ["Have You Heard About the Four Spiritual Laws?"] that you guys let me keep when we came over...I will keep looking for it. I can't remember what it said but I wanted to share it with my friend that I told you about that was having a hard time believing. I've been talking to him a lot about it and actually it isn't going very well. I feel like I'm at a loss....We get into heated discussions and I feel as though I am having to defend the fact that I believe. I told him that seeing isn't believing and even if there was an evolution that many believe created this world that we live in, someone or something had to start it and that someone was god. I told him that you could look at all the theories in the world and trace them back to the smallest atom that you believe created it all and find out that that was god's doing. Or if you think that the atom was a chemical reaction of some kind, then that was god's doing. Maybe I'm not explaining it right, maybe I don't know how to do it, I don't know what to do or how to do it. It seems that the only thing I can do is pray on it. What should I do?"

We wrote back, sent her another copy of the tract, and gave her some additional suggestions to help her with her personal evangelism efforts with her friend.

As I write this, two sailors come to mind. Both recently got out of the Navy. One left to attend college, and the other to work with veterans in his home state. Both of them committed their lives to Christ while they were involved in our ministry, and I had the privilege of baptizing them in water. While they were here we played together, studied the Bible together and prayed together. Now that they are gone, our personal and spiritual conversations continue through Facebook posts, text messages, and phone and video calls.

In 2017, one of the sailors got married. Yvonne and I drove to his home state to perform the wedding ceremony. Our family ties with them continue to grow as well. In March of this year, the couple welcomed their first baby into the world. Which gives us a new adopted grandchild.

In the vision the Lord gave us for this ministry He said, *"All your sons will be taught by the Lord, and great will be your children's peace."*[99]

God continues to work in the hearts and lives of the young men and women He brought into our home. He gave Yvonne and me the privilege of having a part in that work. And as we continue to love them, pray for them, stay in touch, and communicate with them, we believe God will continue to work in their lives, and allow us to continue ministering to them as well.

---

[99] Isaiah 54:13.

12

THE CONTINUING STORY...

Though this is the end of our book, it is not the end of the story. Ministry to the military is an ongoing process. The goal of which is to help young military men and women come to know Jesus Christ as their Lord and Savior. It continues with helping them understand and grow in their faith in Christ, and connect that faith to their lifestyle and behavior. An essential part of that growth is helping them receive the baptism with the Holy Spirit to divinely empower them to be strong and competent witnesses for Jesus Christ wherever they go, for the rest of their lives.

As I write, I think of 1 Corinthians 3:5-8, where Paul says that God gives everyone their own unique role to play in the evangelism process. He said,

> *What, after all, is Apollos? And what is Paul? Only servants, through whom you came to believe—as the Lord has assigned to each his task. I planted the seed, Apollos watered it, but God has been making it grow. So neither the one who plants nor the one who waters is anything, but only God, who makes things grow. The one who plants and the one who waters have one purpose,*

You Invited Me In...

and they will each be rewarded according to their own labor.[100]

Yvonne and I have planted seeds of faith in many young lives. In others, we've watered seeds that had been planted by others before we came along. And there will be those who water the seeds we have planted. We have also had the privilege of harvesting or reaping where others have planted and watered. As I am sure in the future there will be those who harvest where Yvonne and I have planted and watered.

Ultimately, God deserves all the credit for bringing us into contact with the sailors, soldiers, and marines initially. And for giving them the desire to come to our home the first time, and for many, to come back. Yvonne and I are thankful for the relationships that have grown between us and these young men and women and their families. And, we give Him all the credit and glory for the spiritual fruit that is being produced—in them—and through them.

For God *is* producing fruit through those we have reached for Him. As the young men and women we have ministered to in our home share their faith with their shipmates, or others they come in contact with around the world, they too are planting, watering, and harvesting seeds of faith in other people's lives.

We believe what God said to us in Isaiah 55:10-11, that His word and this vision would be fulfilled. He said,

> *As the rain and the snow come down from heaven, and do not return to it without watering the earth and making it bud and flourish, so that it yields seed for the sower and bread for the eater, so is my word that goes out from my mouth: It will not return to me empty, but will*

---

[100] 1 Corinthians 3:5-8.

The Continuing Story...

accomplish what I desire and achieve the purpose for which I sent it.

God continues to work in the hearts and lives of the young men and women who have been in our home, whether they came once or many times. As this passage says, God's Word will not return to Him empty. The seeds that have been planted and watered will one day bear fruit. Those who felt welcome and loved, who enjoyed themselves, and who heard the gospel of Jesus Christ, will one day understand and believe.

This promise also extends to the young men who shared their faith with their shipmates, often in the face of intense opposition. Our efforts and theirs are not and were not wasted. God sees and is making sure that His word is fulfilled!

God told us to write the vision and make it plain on "tablets" so that the person who reads it can run with it. We've done our best to write the vision and make it plain. We now commit this tablet to the Lord and trust that He will do with it what He pleases.

Our hope is that others will see the need and feel God call them to open their homes to young men and women serving in the armed forces of our country. Obviously, the need is great! And as Jesus told His disciples in Matthew 9:37,[101] Yvonne and I pray that the Lord will send laborers into His harvest field.

If you would like to communicate or connect with us there are several ways you can do that. You can visit our website and see the pictures of the servicemen and women involved in our ministry. You can study your Bible using our interactive online Bible studies. There are podcasts of some of my Bible studies and sermons that you can listen to. And there are articles on various topics that I've written that you can read. All of these

---

[101] Matthew 9:37.

You Invited Me In...

online resources are free. Our website address is: http://lighthousemilitaryministry.org

You can also go to our Blog and see the weekly pictures and stories we post of our ongoing activities. There, you can also read testimonies from some of our "sons" and "daughters". Our Blog address is: http://johnandyvon.blogspot.com/

After you've finished this book, seen the pictures, listened to some of the podcasts, done some of the Bible studies, and read some of the testimonies, our hope is that you will have developed an interest in and a burden for our work. So, when you think about us, please pray for us and for the young men and women you've seen in the pictures.

As you can imagine, there are expenses involved in this ministry. If you would like to partner with us and help us financially in this work, you will find a link at the top of our website that will allow you to donate on line. You can also contribute the old fashioned way, with a paper check!

If you have questions about anything you've read we would be happy to communicate with you personally. Our email address is: wagner@lighthousemilitaryministry.org.

Finally, if our story has touched your heart, and inspired you to open *your* home to minister to military men and women in *your* area, Yvonne and I would be glad to help you.

If you're a pastor and would like to begin a Pentecostal hospitality house military ministry in your church we would love to help you do that. We will be glad to discuss this with you and answer any questions you may have. Yvonne and I are also available to come share our vision with you and your people if you would like us to do that.

So for now, God bless and remember to...*invite them in!*

www.ingramcontent.com/pod-product-compliance
Lightning Source LLC
Chambersburg PA
CBHW020852090426
42736CB00008B/350